Broadway Christian Church

Boundaries With Kids When to Say Y...
Cloud, Dr. Henry and Townsend, Dr. John

0000   5909

Resources by Henry Cloud and John Townsend

Boundaries
Boundaries Workbook
Boundaries audio
Boundaries video curriculum
Boundaries with Kids
Boundaries with Kids audio
Changes That Heal (Cloud)
Changes That Heal Workbook (Cloud)
Changes That Heal audio (Cloud)
Hiding from Love (Townsend)
The Mom Factor
The Mom Factor Workbook
The Mom Factor audio
Safe People
Safe People Workbook
Safe People audio
Twelve "Christian" Beliefs That Can Drive You Crazy

BOUNDARIES
with Kids

When to Say YES,

When to Say NO

to Help Your Children
Gain Control of Their Lives

Dr. Henry Cloud
Dr. John Townsend

ZondervanPublishingHouse
Grand Rapids, Michigan

A Division of HarperCollinsPublishers

Boundaries with Kids
Copyright © 1998 by Henry Cloud and John Townsend

Requests for information should be addressed to:

ZondervanPublishingHouse
Grand Rapids, Michigan 49530

Library of Congress Cataloging-in-Publication Data

Cloud, Henry.
 Boundaries with kids : when to say yes, when to say no to help your children gain control of their lives / Henry Cloud and John Townsend.
  p. cm.
 ISBN: 0-310-20035-0 (hardcover)
 1. Discipline of children—United States. 2. Self-control in children—United States. 3. Parenting—United States. I. Townsend, John Sims, 1952– . II. Title.
HQ770.4.C55 1998
649'.64—dc21

98-10491
CIP

This edition is printed on acid-free paper and meets the American National Standards Institute Z39.48 standard.

All Scripture quotations, unless otherwise indicated, are taken from the Holy Bible: New International Version®. NIV®. Copyright © 1973, 1978, 1984 by International Bible Society. Used by permission of Zondervan Publishing House. All rights reserved.

All rights reserved. No part of this publication may be reproduced, stored in a retrieval system, or transmitted in any form or by any means—electronic, mechanical, photocopy, recording, or any other—except for brief quotations in printed reviews, without the prior permission of the publisher.

Published in association with Sealy M. Yates, Literary Agent, Orange, CA.

Interior design by Sue Vandenberg Koppenol

Printed in the United States of America

98 99 00 01 02 03 04 /❖ DC/ 10 9 8 7 6 5 4

Contents

Part 3: Implementing Boundaries with Kids

Introduction

Why Boundaries with Kids

"What is this new book you and Henry are writing?" asked my seven-year-old son, Ricky.

"It's about boundaries and kids," I (Dr. Townsend) replied.

Ricky thought a moment, then said reflectively, "I like to *say* boundaries, but I don't like to *hear* them."

Join the rest of the human race, Ricky. All of us like to set boundaries, but we don't like to hear other people's boundaries. We have empathy for whatever led you, the reader, to pick up this book, because Ricky's statement describes the position of all children (and many adults): What gratifies me is "good" and what frustrates me is "bad." Ever since the time of Adam and Eve, taking ownership of our lives and accepting responsibility for ourselves is something we have resisted. Your task as a parent is to help your child develop inside him what you have been providing on the outside: responsibility, self-control, and freedom. Setting and maintaining boundaries is not an easy task, but with the right ingredients, it really works.

Why Boundaries with Kids?

Several years ago, we coauthored *Boundaries: When to Say Yes, When to Say No to Take Control of Your Life* (Zondervan, 1992). This book sets forth the concept that setting limits helps us better own our lives and, ultimately, helps us love God and others better. The book's ongoing popularity speaks to the need of so many people who struggle with problems such as irresponsible, manipulative, or controlling relationships, emotional issues, work conflicts, and the like.

Since *Boundaries* was published, many parents have asked us questions— in the counseling office, in seminars, and on the radio— about how boundaries work in child rearing. Parents are concerned with raising kids who are not only loving, but also responsible. And they want something that will do more than help people heal broken boundaries. They want something to prevent boundary problems, to help build boundaries in children. This book is for them. It applies the principles in *Boundaries* to the specific context of child rearing.

Who Should Read This Book?

Boundaries with Kids was written for parents of children of all ages, from infancy to the teen years. However, if you aren't a parent, *Boundaries with Kids* may also help you to help the children you love and whose lives you impact. This book will help you if you are a

- Teacher
- Grandparent
- Coach
- Neighbor
- Day-care worker or baby-sitter
- Church youth worker
- Or even a teen who is working on your own boundaries!

Although you may not be a parent, you still want to be a force for responsibility and righteousness in the lives of the kids you influence. This book is designed to help you implement these principles, whether you are a primary caretaker or play a secondary role in a child's life.

Why Should You Read This Book?

You don't have to be in a crisis to benefit from this book. The principles offered here apply to all situations. Your child may be at age-appropriate levels of maturity at home, at school, and in relationships. As a result, you may want to use this material to ensure that the process continues as your child navigates from one age group to another and into adulthood.

But *Boundaries with Kids* will also help with problems and crises in parenting. All parents have problems. Some problems are oriented around issues of responsibility and self-control. This book shows how to deal with these sorts of problems:

- Impulsivity
- Inattention to parental directives
- Defying authority
- Whining
- Procrastination
- Inability to finish tasks
- Aggressive behavior
- School problems
- Conflicts with friends
- Sexual involvement
- Drugs
- Gangs

While this book addresses these and many other problems, it is not "problem centered," but rather "principle centered." By "principle centered" we mean that the book is organized around key concepts that will help children take ownership of their lives. We have taken these concepts from our study of the Bible and God's teaching on responsibility, stewardship, and self-control. In *Boundaries,* the chapter on the Ten Laws of Boundaries was designed to help readers take charge of their lives. In the present book, each law has been expanded to an entire chapter and applied to child rearing.

Boundaries with Kids isn't written chronologically, with separate sections on infancy, toddlerhood, childhood, and the teen years. We organized the book the way we did because we believe the principles of boundaries with children are universal, and they work with kids at all levels of development. You need to apply the laws to your child in age- and maturity-appropriate ways. So we have included in each chapter many examples and illustrations of how these laws are applied at all age levels, to give you a way to understand them in your own situation.

This book is geared much more toward how you, the parent, behave with your child than toward educating your child. Learning boundaries has a lot to do with going through experiences, such as receiving consequences for behavior, learning to take ownership, and dealing with the boundaries of others. It's a lot like how the Bible describes the growth process: "No discipline seems pleasant at the time, but painful. Later on, however, it produces a harvest of righteousness and peace for those who have been trained by it" (Hebrews 12:11).

As you learn to require responsibility from your child, your child learns the value of being responsible. The process begins with you.

Outline of the Book

Boundaries with Kids is organized in three sections. Part 1, "Why Kids Need Boundaries," is an overview of the importance of helping children learn to take responsibility. It describes what a maturing child with boundaries looks like, as well as how a parent with her own boundaries behaves and relates. Part 2, "Ten Boundary Principles Kids Need to Know," deals with each of the ten laws of boundaries. Here you learn that it's not just *teaching* children boundaries, it's *being* a boundary, with consequences, that helps the child learn that his life is his own problem, not yours. Finally, Part 3, "Implementing Boundaries with Kids," concludes the book with six steps of how to implement boundary setting specifically and practically with your child.

Finally, if you are overwhelmed with the task of teaching a young person who sees responsibility as something to be avoided at all costs, be comforted. God is also a parent and for many years has gone through the same pains you are experiencing. He understands, and he will guide and help your willing heart: "The LORD watches over the way of the righteous" (Psalm 1:6). Ask him for his help, wisdom, and resources as you continue the process of helping young people grow up into maturity in him.

So welcome to *Boundaries with Kids*! Our prayer is that you will find help, information, and hope to help your children learn when to say yes and when to say no to take control of their lives.

Part 1

Need Boundaries

April Memory Verse

It is by grace you have been saved, not by works (Ephesians 2:8-9).

— 1 —

The Future Is Now

It was a normal day, but one that would forever change my friend's parenting.

We had finished dinner, and I (Dr. Cloud) was visiting with my friend, Allison, and her husband, Bruce, when she left the dinner table to do some chores. Bruce and I continued to talk until a phone call took him away as well, so I went to see if I could lend Allison a hand.

I could hear her in their fourteen-year-old son Cameron's room. I walked in to a scene that jolted me. She was cheerfully putting away clothes and sports equipment and making the bed. She struck up a conversation as if things were normal: "I can't wait for you to see the pictures from our trip. It was so much—"

"What are you doing?" I asked.

"I'm cleaning up Cameron's room," she said. "What does it look like I'm doing?"

"You are what?"

"I told you. I'm cleaning up his room. Why are you looking at me like that?"

All I could do was to share with her the vision in my head. "I just feel sorry for Cameron's future wife."

Allison straightened up, froze for a moment, and then hurried from the room. I walked into the hall to see her standing there motionless. Not knowing what to say, I said nothing. After a few moments, she looked at me and said, "I've never thought about it that way."

Nor have most of us. We parent in the present without thinking about the future. We usually deal with the problems at hand. Making it through an afternoon without wanting to send our children to an eight-year camp in Alaska seems like a huge accomplishment! But one goal of parenting is to keep an eye on the future. We are raising our children to be responsible adults.

Parents interact with their children in a way that comes naturally to them. For example, Allison was by nature a "helper," and she gladly helped her son. Others have different parenting styles. Some, who are more laid back and uninvolved, leave their son's room alone. Those who are stricter inflict heavy punishment for a less than regulation-made bed.

Certainly, child rearing requires many different interventions. There are times for helping, for not getting involved, or for being strict. But the real issue is this: *Is what you are doing being done on purpose?* Or are you doing it from reasons that you do not think about, such as your own personality, childhood, need of the moment, or fears?

Remember, parenting has to do with more than the present. You are preparing your child for the future. *A person's character is one's destiny.*

A person's character largely determines how he will function in life. Whether he does well in love and in work depends on the abilities he possesses inside. In a world that has begun to explain away people's behavior with a variety of excuses, people are left wondering why their lives do not work. *Most of our problems result from our own character weakness.* Where we possess inner strength, we succeed, often in spite of tough circumstances. But where we do not possess inner strength, we either get stuck or fail. If a relationship requires understanding and forgiveness and we do not have that character ability, the relationship will not make it. If a difficult time period in work requires patience and delay of gratification and we do not possess those traits, we will fail. Character is almost everything.

The word *character* means different things to different people. Some people use *character* to mean moral functioning or integrity. We use the word to describe a person's entire makeup, who he is. Character refers to a person's ability and inability, his moral makeup, his functioning in relationships, and how he does tasks. What does he do in certain situations, and how does he do it? When he needs to perform, how will he meet those demands? Can he love? Can he be responsible? Can he have empathy for others? Can he develop his talents? Can he solve problems? Can he deal with failure? How does he reflect the image of God? These are a few of the issues that define character.

If a person's character makeup determines his future, then child rearing is primarily about helping children to develop character that will take them through life safely, securely, productively, and joyfully. Parents—and those who work with children—would do well to keep this in mind. A major goal of raising children is to help them develop the character that will make their future go well.

It wasn't until Allison saw this future reality that her parenting changed. She loved helping Cameron. But in many ways her helping was not "helping" Cameron. He had developed a pattern in which he felt entitled to everyone else's help, and this feeling of entitlement affected his relationships at school and at church. Allison had always been glad to help Cameron through the messes he was creating. Another undone project was another opportunity to love him.

Yet Allison was not only a mother, but also a grown woman and a wife. When she looked into the future and saw a time when Cameron would be leaving responsibilities for others to do, she became concerned. What a mother doesn't mind doing, others deplore. She glimpsed the reality of character destiny. And she changed how she interacted with Cameron to help him develop a sense of responsibility, to help him think about how his behavior affected others and whether or not others would want to be a part of his future.

It is in this sense that we say the future is now. When you are a parent, you help create a child's future. The patterns children establish early in life (their character) they will live out later. And character is always formed in relationship. We can't overestimate your role in developing this character. As Proverbs says,

"Train a child in the way he should go, and when he is old he will not turn from it" (Proverbs 22:6).

Preventive Medicine

In 1992 we wrote *Boundaries*, a book about taking control of one's life. In *Boundaries* we talked about how to repair the brokenness in character caused by a lack of boundaries. Since that time, through workshops and on radio and television, we have spoken to more than a million people about creating boundaries in their lives. Thousands have told us that creating boundaries has enabled them to love and to live better, some for the first time. Nothing is more exciting than to see people grow and change.

But from our own experience and that of our audiences and readers, one thing became obvious to us. Adults with boundary problems had not developed those problems as grown-ups. They had learned patterns early in life and then continued those out-of-control patterns in their adult lives, where the stakes were higher. They had learned the following boundary problems as youngsters:

- Inability to say no to hurtful people or set limits on hurtful behavior from others
- Inability to say no to their own destructive impulses
- Inability to hear no from others and respect their limits
- Inability to delay gratification and accomplish goals and tasks
- Tendency to be attracted to irresponsible or hurtful people and then try to "fix" them
- Taking responsibility for other people's lives
- Ability to be easily manipulated or controlled
- Struggles with intimacy and maintaining closeness with others
- Inability to be honest with those they are close to
- Inability to confront others and resolve conflicts productively
- Experiencing life as a victim instead of living it purposefully with a feeling of self-control

• Addictions and compulsions
• Disorganization and lack of follow-through

So we began to think preventively. We love helping adults with boundary problems that have gone on for years, but we also want to help children avoid experiencing what many of us had to go through to repair boundary deficits. This realization led us to write this book on boundaries with kids. Most of the adults we encountered had had well-intentioned parents. But many times these parents had had no clue about how to build boundaries into their children; thus they passed on their own limited boundary functioning. Had many of these parents known how to raise a child with good boundaries, much pain could have been prevented. We hope this book will help you to develop the kind of character in your children that will prevent many problems with which adults struggle.

In addition, parents began to ask for this book. They knew the pain they had been through and did not want their children to go through the same kind of learning curve. It is better for a child to lose privileges than for an adult to lose a marriage or a career. In addition, they realized that boundaries are a key to making any relationship work, and they wanted to know how to live out the principles of boundaries with their children. Their questions can be grouped into three basic areas:

• How do I teach boundaries to children?
• How do I enforce my own boundaries with my children in appropriate ways?
• How can I ensure that my children will not have the problems with boundaries that I have had?

We want to help you answer those questions and to help your children develop the character that will lead them into the life that God created them to have.

Children Are Not Born with Boundaries

A boundary is a "property line" that defines a person; it defines where one person ends and someone else begins. If we know where a person's boundaries are, we know what we can expect this person to take control of: himself or herself. We can require responsibility in regard to feelings, behaviors, and attitudes. We have all seen couples, for example, arguing with each other about "who's to blame," each avoiding responsibility for oneself. In a relationship with someone, we can define what we expect of each other, and then we can require each other to take responsibility for our respective part. When we each take ownership for our part of a relationship, the relationship works, and we all accomplish our goals.

A child is no different. A child needs to know where she begins, what she needs to take responsibility for, and what she does not need to take responsibility for. If she knows that the world requires her to take responsibility for her own personhood and life, then she can learn to live up to those requirements and get along well in life.

But if she grows up in a relationship where she is confused about her own boundaries (what she is responsible for) and about others' boundaries (what they are responsible for), she does not develop the self-control that will enable her to steer through life successfully. She will grow up with confused boundaries that lead to the opposite: *trying to control others and being out of control of herself.* In fact, an accurate description of children is that they are little people who are out of control of themselves and attempting to control everyone around them. They do not want to take control of themselves to adapt to the requirements of Mom and Dad; they want Mom and Dad to change the requirements!

You can see why parenting is so difficult. Children are not born with boundaries. They internalize boundaries from external relationships and discipline. In order for children to learn who they are and what they are responsible for, their parents have to have clear boundaries with them and relate to them in ways that help them learn their own boundaries.

If boundaries are clear, children develop several qualities:

- A well-defined sense of who they are
- What they are responsible for

- The ability to choose
- The understanding that if they choose well, things will go well, and if they choose poorly, they will suffer
- The possibility for true love based in freedom

The essence of boundaries is self-control, responsibility, freedom, and love. These are the bedrock of the spiritual life. Along with loving and obeying God, what could be a better outcome of parenting than that? But the question is, how does that happen?

The Three Roles of a Parent

Parenting can be looked at in many different ways. Some see a parent as a coach, some as a police officer, some as a friend, some as God. In part, all of these roles have some truth to them.

In our view, the parent or caretaker role consists of these three main functions:

- Guardian
- Manager
- Source

Guardian

A guardian is legally responsible for a child and, in that capacity, protects and preserves the child. Why does a parent need to provide protection and preservation?

The Bible says that children are "under guardians and managers" until the appropriate time (Galatians 4:2 NASB). Children do not possess the wisdom for protecting and preserving their own lives. They do not know right from wrong, dangerous from safe, good from better, life from death. They think not about the outcome of their actions, but about immediate gratification. Therefore, as they explore and discover their limits, they put themselves in danger. Wisdom comes only from experience—the big thing a child is short on.

A guardian provides the child with a safe environment for learning and gaining wisdom. Too little freedom to gain experience, and the child forever remains a child. Too much freedom, and the child is in danger of hurting himself. So balancing freedom and limits becomes a major task in child rearing. Parents must guard children from danger, protect them from harm, and preserve their lives.

This protective guardian steps in with appropriate boundaries and limits to guard children from several sources of danger:

1. Dangers within themselves
2. Dangers in the outside world
3. Inappropriate freedoms that they are not ready to handle
4. Never appropriate or evil actions, behaviors, or attitudes (such as serial killing or using LSD)
5. Their own regressive tendency to remain dependent and avoid growing up

Parents, in their role as guardian, keep the child safe, growing, and healthy. More often than not, they use boundaries to perform this function. They set limits to freedom, and then enforce them for the child's protection. Through this process, the child internalizes the limits as wisdom and slowly begins to be able to take care of herself.

Manager

A manager makes sure things get done—goals are reached, demands and expectations are met. Children are not born with self-discipline; therefore they have to have "other-discipline." Managers provide this other-discipline by making sure the child does the tasks at hand to meet the expectations important for her growth.

Managers provide this discipline by controlling resources, teaching, enforcing consequences, correcting, chastising, maintaining order, and building skills. They oversee the day-to-day hard work of reaching goals.

When Allison decided that she was going to guard Cameron from his wish to avoid being responsible for himself, she had to manage that process. As you may suspect, Cameron did not immediately sign up for the new plan! Allison had to set some goals, control the resources, and manage the consequences until her son developed the discipline that he would eventually need to get along well with someone other than Mom. In short, she had to manage his immaturity. For instance, she gave him time lines to learn to take care of his belongings and perform jobs around the house. She outlined what would happen if he did not, and she stuck to the consequences that she promised to impose. He lost many privileges and learned the cost of being a slacker.

Boundaries play an important role in managing. Setting limits and requiring the child to take ownership (embracing the problem as his own) and responsibility (taking care of what he has embraced) entail a clear understanding of boundaries. We will talk more about this later.

Source

Children come into the world without resources. They don't know where the food is, how to get shelter, or how to obtain the money they need for basic supplies. They have immaterial needs as well, without knowing how to meet them. They need love, spiritual growth, wisdom, support, and knowledge, all of which are out of their reach.

Parents are the source of all good things for a child. They are the bridge to the outside world of resources that sustain life. And in giving and receiving resources, boundaries play a very important role. Children need to learn how to receive and use responsibly what is given them and gradually take over the role of meeting their own needs. In the beginning, parents are the source; they progressively give the child the independence to obtain what they need on their own.

Being the source for children is fraught with blessing and difficulty. If parents give without boundaries, children learn to feel entitled and become self-centered and demanding. Ungratefulness becomes a character pattern. If parents hold resources too tightly, children give up and do not develop the hope of reaching goals that have gratifying rewards. We will see how boundaries help structure the resources and how they play an important role in parenting.

Learning to Take Responsibility

When Cameron was first enlisted in the process of learning how to take responsibility for cleaning up, he was lacking several things:

- He did not feel the need to clean up. Mom felt that need.
- He did not feel motivated to clean up. Mom felt motivated.
- He did not plan for or take the time to clean up. Mom did.
- He did not have the skill to organize. Mom did.

So how did he learn to take responsibility for himself? There was a slow transfer of these qualities from the outside of Cameron to the inside. Whereas Mom possessed all the qualities inside of her and Cameron did not, boundaries reversed all that. In the end, Mom did not feel the need or the motivation, and she did not take the time or use her skills. Instead, Cameron did. Boundaries facilitated the process of having the child internalize things that were external to him. And in the final analysis, building boundaries in a child accomplishes this: *What was once external becomes internal.*

In the rest of this book we will talk about the process by which kids internalize the structure they do not naturally possess. As you take a stance of good clear boundaries with children, they will have a better chance of gaining the motivation, the need, the skill, and the plan to live a loving, responsible, righteous, and successful life unto God and others. And this is what character is all about.

In the next chapter we will take a closer look at the kind of character we want to develop in our children.

— 2 —

What Does Character Look Like?

When Allison visualized her son Cameron's marriage, she could see that responsibility for oneself was an important quality to build into her child. She changed her focus from dealing with the immediate moment to thinking about long-term character development. What kind of person was she teaching Cameron to be?

Surely, we want our children to be responsible. But often we don't have a very clear picture of the character we are trying to build. In dealing with children, we are sometimes trying to get through the day, or sometimes the next hour! But if we could look ahead to the person we are trying to develop, then we could get a handle on some of the immediate parenting problems. It is essential to realize that when you get Johnny to do his homework, it is not just about getting that assignment done; it is about the possible success or failure of his marriage or career. That is why we want you to take a brief tour with us into the life of "Johnny twenty years later." In this chapter we would like to give you some qualities we consider important to adult functioning, qualities in which boundaries play an essential developing role.

Loving

Out of the three great virtues of faith, hope, and love, the apostle Paul wrote that "the greatest of these is love" (1 Corinthians 13:13). Most parents would say that they want their children to be loving.

Loving people recognize that the world does not revolve around them. They consider the consequences of their behavior on people around them before they act. In psychological terms, they are not "egocentric"—thinking that they are all that matters and that people around them exist only to meet their demands and needs.

But sometimes the most loving parents end up with the most selfish children. How can that be? We have all heard people say things like, "You know how Susan is. She only thinks of herself." And many times, Susan comes from a nice family. But Susan's parents did not set boundaries that required her to respect the feelings of others. This lack of boundaries led to egocentrism, which affected Susan's ability to love. Having no boundaries in childhood can also lead to impulse problems, addictions, or irresponsibility, which is always unloving.

George sat in my (Dr. Cloud's) office, despondent. His wife, Janet, whom he loved deeply, had just moved out because he had lost another job. A very talented person, George seemed to have everything he needed for success. But he had lost several good jobs because of his irresponsibility and inability to follow through. Bosses loved the talent but hated the performance. And after several family disruptions because of his failures, Janet had had enough.

"I love her so much," George said to me. "Doesn't she see that?"

"I believe that you love her," I said. "But in reality, I don't think that she does see your love. All she sees is the effect your behavior has had on her and the children, and she asks herself, 'How can he love us and treat us this way?' You cannot just love someone and not deliver. Love without the fruits of love is really not love in the end. She feels very unloved because of what you have put her through."

If George was to have a chance of winning Janet back, it would not come through one more empty promise. He needed to develop boundaries to gain the self-control that would make him a responsible person. Janet was only going to believe in action, not just talk about love.

George had never been required to deliver the fruits of love when growing up. His parents were fine, hardworking people. But having gone through the Depression and a lifetime of hard work, they did not want George to have to struggle as they had. As a result, they indulged him and required very little work from him. When they did give him chores and responsibilities and he did not deliver, they would not discipline him, thinking that they wanted him to have "positive self-esteem" rather than the "guilt" with which they grew up. Consequently, he did not see any negative effect on his loved ones when he did not perform.

But marriage was different. He was now in a relationship in which the one he loved also had requirements for him, and things were falling apart. For George to become a truly loving person, one whose love actually made a difference in the lives of others, he was going to have to become a responsible person. In the end, love is as love does.

Moreover, loving people respect the boundaries of others. Have you ever been in a relationship with a person who could not hear the word no? How did you feel? Typically one feels controlled, manipulated, and resentful instead of respected and loved. A controlling person steps over the line and tries to possess the other. This does not feel very loving, no matter how much the offender says he cares.

Loving people are able to control their impulses. Many alcoholics, for example, have great love for their families. Their drinking greatly troubles them, and they feel horrendous guilt. But still they drink, and although, like George, they love, the effects of their lack of ability to say no to alcohol ends up destroying the relationships they care about. Many other impulse problems—such as sexual acting out, overspending, food or drug abuse, and rage attacks—end up destroying love as well. A lack of boundaries keeps these behaviors going.

Responsible

Another aspect of mature character is responsibility. George's irresponsibility was costing him his marriage and had cost him financial losses, chaos, a lack of stability, and unrealized dreams.

But what is this thing we call responsibility? Many things come to mind, such as duty or obligations, reliability and dependability, or just "getting the job done."

Responsibility is actually broader than this. We think of responsibility in terms of ownership. To take ownership of your life is ultimately to take control. Ownership is to truly possess your life and to know that you are accountable for your life—to God and others. When you take ownership, you realize that all aspects of your life are truly yours and only yours, and that no one is going to live your life for you.

We shall all give an account to God for our lives (2 Corinthians 5:10), and he will hold us responsible for what we did with our talents, resources, relationships, time, and actions. People who are accountable see life as something that has been entrusted to them, and they know that they and they only will be responsible for what they do with it.

In the book *Boundaries* we wrote about what falls within our boundaries, what our boundaries define and protect. Truly responsible people take ownership for the following things:

- Feelings
- Attitudes
- Behaviors
- Choices
- Limits
- Talents
- Thoughts
- Desires
- Values
- Loves

To take ownership of these is to be a truly responsible person, the kind of person with whom everyone wants to have a relationship. A responsible person says, "My feelings are *my* problem," or "My attitude is *my* problem."

Responsibility has been problematic for humankind ever since the Garden of Eden. Remember how Adam did not take responsibility for his own choices? When God asked him what had happened, he blamed Eve. "It was the woman you gave me," he said, implicating not only Eve, but God as well—as if God and Eve were to blame for his wrong choice! And then Eve blamed the serpent for deceiving her. The human race has been struggling with such lack of ownership ever since. And if we cannot take ownership of our lives, we are not in control of them either.

The other day I was counseling a couple who were having marital problems. I asked each of them about their behavior.

"Why do you withdraw from him?" I asked the wife.

"Because he yells at me," she replied.

"Why do you yell?" I asked the husband.

"Because she withdraws from me," he answered.

My question to them at this point was simple: "How long do you think this can go on?"

Both of them told me that they couldn't control their own behavior. Each thought their problems were the other one's fault. With each one disowning their own behavior toward the other, there was little chance for change. They reminded me of Adam and Eve.

Your goal for your child is that he will gradually learn that what falls within his boundaries—feelings, attitudes, and behaviors— are his problem, not someone else's. The child who says of his sister, "She made me do it," will be saying the same thing as an adult. The truly responsible adult realizes, "I made me do it, and I am responsible." With that, there is hope for self-control to develop.

Free

Have you ever been in a relationship with a "victim"? Victims feel as if they have no choices in life. Life is something that happens to them, and whatever comes their way is their lot.

A woman complained to me about a coworker who would always interrupt her while she was trying to get her job done. She acted as if her tendency to be behind in her work was her coworker's fault.

"Why do you talk to her?" I asked.

"What do you mean?"

"When she comes in and interrupts, why do you get into a conversation with her?"

"Well, I have to. She is standing there talking."

"Why don't you just tell her that you have work to do, or close your door and put up a 'Do Not Disturb' sign?"

The woman looked at me with a blank stare. To have choices and to have control of her own behavior was a concept that hadn't occurred to her. She felt that if something happened "to her," then that was the way it had to be. There was nothing she could do to change it. When I suggested that she had many choices, she quizzed me about them. I gave her five or six suggestions, from talking to the woman about the problem, to talking to a supervisor, to asking to be moved to another area. This was a totally new way of thinking for her; she had never learned that she was free to make choices in relationships and in life.

Joe was such a victim. His company was imposing some new policies that he found difficult to handle, and he was very depressed about the changes.

"What are you going to do about it?" I asked him.

"What do you mean, *do* about it?" Joe asked.

"I mean what are you going to do about your being stuck in something you don't like?"

He just looked at me. It took a long time before he realized that he could choose to get his resume out to some other firms and not be a victim to the fifty-hour workweek he hated.

Children raised with good boundaries learn that they are not only responsible for their lives, but also free to live their lives any way they choose, as long as they take responsibility for their choices. For the responsible adult, the sky is the limit.

We live in a society of victims. People today act as if they have no choices in life and that everything should be done for them. If it's not, they can't do it themselves or make changes. This presents a big opportunity for the future: If you raise your children to take control of their own lives, they will be so far ahead of everyone else that success in life is all but guaranteed! What a head start they are going to have on the rest of the pack!

Initiating

Jeri was telling me of her relationship with Dave. She loved his humor, his sensitivity, and his compassion, but she was struggling with his lack of initiative. She and Dave would agree to do something new, such as exercise together, but when it came time to follow through on their plan, nothing would happen unless she took charge. She always felt as if she were "pushing him uphill."

I knew that Dave's boss felt the same way. Dave would eventually do what was required of him, but it always seemed to take some outside force to get him going. People resented his lack of ambition.

A normal part of human behavior is to initiate things. Being created in the image of God is being created with the ability to begin something. Often, a problem with initiating things is a boundary problem. Dave lacked the structure for goal-oriented behavior that boundaries provide.

A child needs to be required to initiate, an important aspect of boundary training. Several years ago, I was with a friend of mine who has a ten-year-old son. While we were talking, Davey came in several times complaining of "nothing to do," wanting his mom to design playtime for him. Knowing that he had all the resources he needed, she looked at him and said, "Davey, you are responsible for your own fun." Not long after that, he found a friend to come over and play.

I recently ran into this mother, and we were catching up on each other's lives. She reported on all the interesting things that Davey was doing now in his last year of college. Inside I thought, *He is still taking responsibility for his own fun.*

"Life is something that happens to us while we are making other plans," says mystery writer Margaret Millar. But for many, life is something they take control of and pursue with diligence. They take their talents and multiply them, ever increasing their involvement in life. They are taking "responsibility for their own fun" and the outcome of their goals. The ones who do not do this are in many cases people who were not required to initiate and complete their tasks and goals; instead someone else did it for them or bailed them out of the consequences of their acts.

Respectful of Reality

Someone once said, "Reality is a tough place to live, but it is the only place to get a good steak." While reality can be tough to handle, it is where the good things of life reside as well. The character that creates a life that works must have a healthy respect for reality. By reality we mean experiencing the consequences of our actions in the real world. We will cover this idea in depth in a later chapter, but for now let's just take a peek at the concept.

In short, every person has to come to the realization that one's actions have real consequences in a real world. People of maturity use this concept to make wonderful lives for themselves, and people of misery beat their heads against it over and over again.

On the positive side, if I study and apply myself, I will reap rewards for my hard work. I recently spent some time with a friend from college. In his sophomore year he had changed his major to premed. I remember watching him work so diligently as he studied organic chemistry, physics, and the like. Already a year and a half behind, he knew that he had some catching up to do. He also knew that hard work and study could get him admitted to medical school. The race was on.

Today this friend is a well-respected heart surgeon in a major metropolitan area. He loves his work and has become a leader in the field of medicine. Many people look up to him and admire his work. When they see this respected heart surgeon, they do not see the college kid who counted on the Law of Reality Consequences: If I study and work hard, I will do well. They only see the fruit of all his work.

When we see great accomplishment, we see only the accomplishment, not what went into it. As a result, we fall prey to magical thinking. We mistakenly think that someone accomplished great things by superhuman abilities or some hidden kind of know-how. We think it was magic. But the reality is that the achievement came one day at a time, one course at a time, one assignment at a time. And we need to teach our children to think that way as well. When they learn this, they learn that they also can accomplish great things. They gain a healthy respect for the positive side of reality.

But reality has two sides. Goofing off and laziness will cost me. Speeding may cost me the use of the car. My behavior has reality consequences. If I realize this, then I work with both hope for reward and a desire to avoid painful realities that may come from my nonperformance or poor choices.

We all know adults who have little respect for reality. They continue to make poor choices, and either they are enabled by others to avoid the consequences of their behavior until a real catastrophe occurs, or they suffer one terrible loss after another. We wonder why they continue to make the same devastating choices.

Time and time again, we can find the roots of such behavior in a lack of those boundaries that would have caused the person to gain a healthy respect for reality. They were bailed out too many times. They were allowed to think that consequences were for someone else and not them.

Mature adults have a healthy respect for reality. They know that, for the most part, if they do good, good things will happen. If they do nothing, or do bad, bad things will happen. This dual respect for the positive and negative sides of reality is often referred to as wisdom.

Of course, bad things do happen to good people. But even then, if one responds with good, the outcome will be better. We always have something to say about the ultimate reality in which we live.

Growing

Have you ever run into a person you haven't seen in some time, and her life is much better than it was before? And you walked away with a certain warm feeling of appreciation for what this person had accomplished? Think of some examples we have all seen:

- Someone has lost sixty pounds.
- A couple on the verge of divorce have put things back together and are doing well.

- Someone with career difficulties has begun to succeed.
- The "black sheep" turns around.
- An addict or alcoholic is living a life of sobriety.
- Someone with a history of heartbreak finds a lasting relationship.

Or if we leave the realm of difficulties and look at normal things getting better, we see the same kind of things:

- Someone begins a small business, and it grows into something big.
- Someone moves across the country with nothing and no one and creates a life for herself.
- A person makes a midlife career change, learns a new craft, and succeeds.
- A shy person develops a circle of friends and close relationships.

Few things inspire us like a story of a person's growing and overcoming some difficult obstacle, especially in her own character. We love to see people change and grow, becoming something that they were not or becoming more of what they were. Movies like *Regarding Henry* and *The Doctor* captivate us because someone changes and grows.

The ability to grow is a character issue. Good parenting can help a child develop character that faces the obstacles of life with an orientation toward growth. It includes developing abilities and gaining knowledge as well as facing negative things about oneself that need changing.

The character that is able to grow includes the ability to

- Recover from distressing emotional states
- Sustain periods of negative strain and delay gratification or good feelings until a responsibility has been met
- Lose well, grieve, and let go of what cannot be reclaimed or won
- Confess when one is wrong
- Change behavior or direction when confronted with reality

- Forgive
- Take ownership of a problem

A person who can do these things is able to grow when presented with a difficult challenge.

I recently acted as a consultant on a personnel problem for a large organization. The person in question was up against a wall; his behavior and performance were not what the organization desired of him. He was enormously talented, but was probably going to lose his position if he did not change. He had recently been promoted to a high level of responsibility in which he managed operations in many states. He had run into trouble when the new responsibilities required some new levels of ability in dealing with problems and people.

For example, he had to resolve conflicts between employees and the home office. Sometimes, whether or not someone quit would depend on how he handled the conflict. But he had problems dealing with people in emotional situations. He became adversarial. In addition, he wanted instant success from these changes.

Instead of responding to the new opportunity and new requirements with an attitude of needing to grow into them, he did the opposite. He demanded that the organization and his bosses change and realize that he was "right." In fact, in looking at the above list of abilities characteristic of a growing person, he fell short in all of them. He acted out difficult feelings instead of resolving them. He couldn't suffer through the losses, let go of them, and plan a course of action. He was not willing to buckle down and implement the kinds of changes that would not bear fruit for a while; he wanted instant results. When confronted, he blamed. When asked to change, he continued on his present course.

In the end, he was replaced with someone of lesser talent but greater character. I was saddened, because if he had had an orientation toward growth, he could have done very well. When I followed up on him, I found patterns of resisting growth that had been present since his childhood. He had never really been required to adapt to the demands of reality. He had always been allowed to stay the way he was; he had used his charm and talent to put off changing.

To avoid wasting this kind of talent, parents need to require their children to do the changing, instead of trying to get reality to change. Boundaries help children see what is expected of them and how they need to grow to meet those expectations.

Oriented to Truth

A less-than-honest person is somewhere between a pain and a catastrophe. As a counselor I have seen more heartache caused by dishonesty than probably any other relationship problem. Dishonesty fuels betrayal, blocks intimacy, and prevents growth. To the extent that a person is able and willing to be honest, he can grow.

Honesty begins with parents who model it, require it from their children, and provide them with a safe environment in which to be honest. By and large, all children hide the truth when it threatens them. So parents need to create a context in which a child's natural tendency to hide can be overcome. This requires a delicate balance between safety and standards.

I had been working with Sara and Tom for a few months when Sara came in one day and said, "It's over. I just cannot trust him, and I never will be able to."

"What happened?" I asked her, thinking that he must have had another affair. He had had one a few years earlier that she had not gotten over.

"He said that we had enough money to pay the bills and not to worry. Then today I got several notices in the mail that we are behind on everything." She started sobbing. "I just cannot live this way any longer."

As we talked about this, I heard a scenario that I had heard literally hundreds of times from spouses with less-than-truthful mates. The sadness was this: *The money problem was not the problem. The problem was that Tom was not honest about the money problem.* Sara could have dealt with the money problem. But because Tom could not be honest about how far behind they were on the bills, Sara was always in quicksand. She was forever finding out that things were not as Tom had led her to believe. The things that spouses lie about are usually not even big things. But hiding and lying always breaks trust. The cry that I usually hear from an injured spouse is something like this: "I don't care what it is, just tell me the real picture so I know what we are dealing with."

The sad question about a liar is why? Why lie when it would be so much easier to tell the truth? Why deceive when it causes much more anger than admission of the mistake would have caused? Why create another problem (lying) when you already have one?

Usually the answer lies in the person's history and character development. He fears anger, shame, guilt, condemnation, and abandonment as a result of his mistake in a relationship. So he hides the truth. Then, when he is found out, he incurs anger, shame, guilt, condemnation, and abandonment—all the things he feared in the first place. But he incurs them more for the lying than for making the mistake.

Boundaries help someone to tell the truth. Besides requiring the truth, boundaries give the safety of known consequences for failure. *Children can handle the known logical consequences of their mistakes, like a time-out, loss of TV privileges, or loss of a trip to the mall, much better than they can handle relational consequences like anger, guilt, shame, condemnation, or abandonment.* Children hide from relational consequences more than the known logical consequences of their behavior.

Oriented to Transcendence

"It is he who made us, and we are his," said the psalmist (Psalm 100:3). The most important questions that anyone has to answer are "Who is God?" and "Is it me, or is it God?" The answers govern every direction of a person's life.

People who know that they are not God look up to God to transcend their own existence. They order their lives around him and his values. They realize they are here not to serve themselves, but him. They understand the greatest commandment: "Love the Lord your God with all your heart and with all your soul and with all your mind" (Matthew 22:37). Being grounded in God gives direction and meaning to their existence, allowing them to transcend life, problems, their own limitations and mistakes, and other people's sins against them. Without an orientation to transcend the realities of this life and touch the realities of God, people are very limited.

One of the saddest things about people without this sense of transcendence is how others experience them. Others continually run into these people's inability to see that they are not God and that life does not revolve around them. Because these people forever build a life around themselves and their own self-centeredness, others feel like objects instead of people. To transcend oneself means to be able to get past one's own existence and value the existence of others. People who do not do this are in some way expecting life and others to serve them, and not the other way around.

People who have the ability to transcend themselves go beyond their own existence to the reality of others, God, and virtues they hold more important than themselves and their own immediate happiness. They are able to delay or forgo immediate gratification for the sake of a higher virtue or value, or for the sake of someone or Someone other than themselves. In short, because they realize that life is bigger than they are, they become bigger than they are at any given moment to meet its demands. Humility makes them larger than they were—the ultimate paradox. Pride brings about destruction, and humility true glory.

A Tall Order

Seeing character building as a task of parenting can be overwhelming. It is certainly easier to manage the moment or to do what comes naturally. But the need is greater and higher. As we said before, a child's character will determine much of the course his life takes.

"Begin with the end in mind," says Stephen Covey in his bestselling book *The Seven Habits of Highly Effective People*. Beginning with the end in mind is a trait of people who do well. It is also a trait of people who parent well. When we understand that a major goal of parents is to develop a person of good character, we have gotten closer to that goal.

But to develop a child of good character, we have to be parents of good character. To develop boundaries in our children, *we* have to have boundaries. And that's the subject of the next chapter.

PROPERTY OF
BROADWAY CHRISTIAN CHURCH LIBRARY
910 BROADWAY
FORT WAYNE, IN 46802

— 3 —

Kids Need Parents with Boundaries

I (Dr. Townsend) first heard the words "problem child" when I was in grade school. I overheard two teachers talking about Wayne, a classmate of mine. "I had heard Wayne was a problem child even before he came to my classroom," one teacher said to her colleague.

Because I knew Wayne, the phrase made sense to me. Although I liked him, he had always seemed out of control. He was disruptive, pushy, intrusive, and sassy with teachers. I didn't think much about why he was that way until I visited his home one Saturday.

Wayne's parents were nice, but they provided very little structure for their son. For example, he and I got too loud while bouncing basketballs in the living room. We did it a long time before anyone said anything. Then his mom came in and said with a pleading smile, "Wayne, dear, I hate to interrupt your fun, but would it be too much trouble to play somewhere else?"

He smarted off to her, and we continued.

After a while, his dad entered the room and blew up at us: "Hey, you guys, how many times do I have to keep telling you to knock it off?"

So we left and continued the dribbling upstairs in Wayne's bedroom, where all those downstairs were driven even more insane. Wayne had the run of the house.

"Problem kids" don't evolve in a vacuum. Every problem child generally has a problem context, and kids with healthy limits don't grow them out of thin air. Although by nature we resist

limits from birth, we have a lot of help either developing boundaries or not developing them. Whenever you begin to look at
where boundary conflicts and development problems come from,
"Look to the rock from which you were cut and to the quarry
from which you were hewn" (Isaiah 51:1).

As both Christians and psychologists, we live in two different environments. The religious world sometimes blames problems on the child, saying that it's all in Suzie's sinful nature. The
counseling world sometimes blames the parents, placing all out-
of-control behaviors on "what happened to Suzie as a child."
In each case, there's a clear good guy and there's a clear bad guy.

Neither of these views is completely accurate. Actually, the
news is worse than that! *Who we are today is essentially the result
of two forces: our environment* and *our responses to it.* Our parenting, significant relationships, and circumstances powerfully
shape our character and attitudes. But how we react to our significant relationships and circumstances—whether defensively
or responsibly—also influences what kind of person we become.

You may have a child with boundary difficulties, or you may
simply want to help your child become a responsible, honest person. Either way, this chapter is not intended to make you feel
guilty. Rather, we want to set out the first and most important
ingredient of helping children learn boundaries: a parent with
boundaries.

Your Child Is Reacting to Your Parenting

Let's not ignore the reality that my friend Wayne had problems. And let's not ignore that the problems were Wayne's and
that he needed to work on them. But there is another principle at work here: *You need to interpret a child's behavior as a
response to your own.* This requires a shift in focus, as we normally look at a person's actions in terms of his motives, needs,
personality, and circumstances, not our own.

Take Wayne, for example. My friend was disrespectful, unre-
sponsive to authority, and out of control. One might attempt
to understand Wayne's behavior in several ways. He is impulsive, self-centered, or immature. These might all be true, but

they don't address his parents. Wayne was responding to his parents' style of relating. He was going as far as they would allow. He knew his mother was impotent and fearful of conflict, so he took advantage of her weakness. He knew that his dad would rant and rave and that he could do what he wanted until Dad blew up. He understood that, even then, he could slide by his father's edict on a technicality and go misbehave somewhere else, as Dad most likely wouldn't follow up with a consequence, preferring instead to go back to his newspaper, feeling justified that he had set that boy straight.

As a rule, children don't know what they are doing. They have little idea how to handle life so that it works right. That's why God gave them parents—to love them, give them structure, and guide them into maturity. So, just as a puppy needs obedience training, kids need help from the outside. Basically, children will mature to the level the parent structures them, and no higher. The parent's limitations in being able to be responsible and teach responsibility influence how well children learn responsibility. Children don't have it in them to grow themselves up. They respond and adapt to how they are parented.

The first and most fundamental mental picture children have of the way the universe operates is at home. The home is where they form their concepts of reality, love, responsibility, choices, and freedom. So if you relate to your children in a way that mirrors God's laws, they will make a successful transition to the outside world. But if you protect your children from the pain of irresponsibility, you set them up for many struggles in adulthood.

One of the most helpful questions parents can ask themselves when faced with a child's problem is not, "Why won't he stop hitting his brother?" but "What was my part in creating this problem?" This may be painful, as it will require your looking at the plank in your eye rather than the speck of sawdust in your child's (see Matthew 7:1–5). But the benefit of this approach is that it takes you out of the futility of trying to control your child and into the possibility that you can control your stance with your child.

Being a parent with boundaries who is developing a child with boundaries requires accepting the reality that *this book is not enough.* Get to work on yourself, too. Find where your own boundaries are weak. Get information and help. If you haven't already read our book *Boundaries,* we suggest you pick up a copy of the book and workbook. A video curriculum is also available for groups. Repair and develop boundaries with God and with the other growing people in your life.

Your Three Avenues of Influence

There are three ways you can influence your kids to develop boundaries.

Teaching

You teach your children to tie their shoes, ride a bike, and clean their rooms. You send them to school to learn a million facts and skills. You can also teach them boundaries—the ability to hear and say no appropriately.

The concepts and principles of boundaries are explicit and clear. They aren't vague, esoteric ideas; instead, they are grounded in reality, God's laws, and everyday life. As a result, you can directly teach boundaries, and your children can learn them. You can help your children put words to their experiences, apply your teaching to new situations, and clarify and modify the teachings as they grow and develop.

For example, don't be afraid to use the word *boundary* with your child; it's a useful one. When she defiantly refuses to stop screaming in anger at you, wait until a calm time later. Then say, "Jill, we have a boundary in this house that screaming is not okay. You can be angry, and talk about your anger at me, but screaming bothers people. If you cross the boundary of screaming, the consequence will be losing playtime after school for that day."

Even further, teach your children boundary principles, not simply practical applications. Young children can learn the statement, "You are responsible for your behavior." This means that they must accept the responsibility for things such as cleaning their room, getting good grades, displaying proper table manners, and controlling tantrums. They will not be able to blame the lack of accomplishment on anyone else. Boundary concepts like these can quickly become part of a family's everyday life, and children will see the applications in other areas. One four-year-old boy has said to his sibling, "Don't take that toy; that's my boundary." Diligently teach these ideas to your children at their age-appropriate level (Deuteronomy 6:6–7).

Here are some broad guidelines for understanding the different boundaries that apply to different age levels in children.

Birth to twelve months. During the first year of life infants are bonding with their mother and father and establishing basic trust, so boundaries at this age should be very minimal. Infants do not have enough love or structure within them to tolerate a great deal of frustration. During this time of learning, the mother needs to protect and nurture and meet the baby's needs for comfort and love.

One to three years. Children at this age can learn to respond to the word *no* and can understand the consequences of their disobedience. This can apply to dangerous situations, tantrums, violence, and more. They may not be able to understand your logic, but they can generally understand that obeying your no brings good things and ignoring your no brings discomfort.

Three to five years. During this period, children are more able to understand the reasons for taking responsibility and what consequences are about. They can talk with you about it. Learning how to treat friends kindly, responding to authority, disagreeing while being respectful, and doing household chores are all a part of defining boundaries at this stage. Consequences such as time-outs and loss of toys, TV, or fun activities are effective at this age.

Six to eleven years. This stage involves a great deal of industriousness as well as an increasing investment in the world outside the family: school, activities, church, and friends. Boundary issues will revolve around balancing time at home and with friends, homework and school tasks, goal orientation, and budgeting time and money. Consequences can involve restrictions on friendships, freedoms, and home privileges.

Twelve to eighteen years. Adolescence is the final step before adulthood. It involves tasks such as solidifying one's identity as distinct from the parents' identity, career leanings, sexual maturation, love choices, and values. It is also the period in which you should begin "de-parenting"—moving from a position of control to one of influence with your child.

When your children are teenagers, help them with issues such as relationships, values, scheduling, and long-term goals. Provide them with as many natural consequences as possible (no money, or supporting the consequences the school metes out, for example).

One thing to remember about this stage: The teen who is acting like a three-year-old should not have the freedoms earned by a mature teen. Freedom comes from handling responsibility well; it is not a gift bequeathed by chronological age.

Modeling

Modeling is different from teaching. Children observe and learn from how you operate with boundaries in your own world. They watch how you treat them, your spouse, and your work. And they emulate you, for good or for bad. They look up to and want to be like these larger, more powerful individuals. By putting on Dad's loafers or Mom's lipstick, they are trying on adult roles to see what fits. In this sense, boundaries are "caught" more than they are "taught."

Modeling goes on all the time, not just when you are in a "parenting" mode. It occurs basically any time you are in eyesight or earshot of the child. Many a mother is dismayed when she finds her children doing what she does, not what she says: "I taught them right from wrong!" she'll exclaim. And she may have, but often her child figured out early in the game how his mother's (or father's) beliefs fit in with her actions.

Universal house rules of conduct are a good example of this. Many rules of privilege and responsibility, such as bedtimes and TV watching, are different for kids and adults; however, some rules should apply to all members of the family. One illustration is the rule, "No one interrupts another person who is talking." Parents often feel that what they have to say is more important than a child's ramblings about what happened at school.

However, if the understanding exists in the family that any member can confront another on a universal rule, the child sees respect for others modeled. When little Jeremy can say, "Mom, you interrupted me," and Mom can respond nondefensively with, "You're right, son. Sorry about that," the child is learning that respect, ownership, apologizing, and responding to house rules are things that grown-ups do.

These are not only good, healthy, or mature aspects of being an adult, but norms of reality. And children are desperately looking for norms on which to hang their hats. That's why, if Mom were instead to say, "Jeremy, you don't understand. What I needed to say had to be said because it was very, very important," Jeremy would be just as likely to become defensive and rationalize his behavior when confronted on infractions. *A child's need to belong is more central than his need to be good.* If obeying house boundaries helps him belong, so be it. If rebelling against them brings him attention and belonging, so be it again. What you model is the key.

Helping Your Child to Internalize

To internalize something is to make it part of yourself. It is more than learning a fact, and different from watching a fact fleshed out. It is making that fact an experienced reality. There are two ways to "know" something: intellectually and experientially. You can memorize a definition of romantic love, an intellectual "knowing." Falling in love, however, is a much different matter, an experienced "knowing."

This difference may dismay you, but if you embrace it, your parenting will flourish: *If your boundary training consists only of words, you are wasting your breath.* But if you "do" boundaries with your kids, they internalize the experiences, remember them, digest them, and make them part of how they see reality.

My wife, Barbi, and I recently began working on financial responsibility with our sons Ricky, seven, and Benny, five. We allotted a small amount of money to them on a weekly basis, based on certain chores they were to do. Part of their income goes to tithing, part to savings, and part is for spending money.

When the process started, the boys thought money grew on trees. They liked having it, but had no sense of fiscal responsibility. To them, it was great having money, and there would always be . more. Barbi and I lectured them several times on saving up for what they wanted and not spending it all at once. It went in one ear and out the other. It was not their fault; they'd simply had no experience with wanting something and being broke.

One day the boys used all their spending money on a toy they wanted. A couple of days later, a comic book they had wanted for a long time went on sale, and they went to their spending pouches. The pouches had not replenished themselves overnight. They were empty. So they went to Mom and Dad for help. We said, "No gifts, no loans. Earn it at the usual weekly rate." They then asked if they could do extra chores. We said no.

Then they cried. We empathized with the loss of the on-sale opportunity, but the pouches stayed empty. A few hours later, Benny said, "I'm going to wait a long, long, long time next time." And he did, and they did. The next payday, they squirreled the spending portion away, talking about how much they were going to save and how little they were going to spend. They had begun to internalize the reality that if you spend it now, you won't have it later.

No amount of lecturing and nagging would have accomplished this result. It took an experience with parental boundaries to develop child boundaries. You are like an oak tree that the child runs her head into over and over again, until she realizes that the tree is stronger than she is, and she walks around it next time.

Obstacles to Teaching Boundaries

"If you can't stand the heat, stay out of the kitchen" goes the old saying. Part of the heat of parenting is tolerating and enduring your child's hatred of your boundaries. You and your child each have a different job here: The kid's job is to test your resolve, so she can learn about reality. Your job is to withstand the test, including anger, pouting, tantrums, and much more. One of the great parenting failures in the Bible is that of King David and his son, Adonijah. Although David was a great leader, he neglected the boundary-setting aspect of child rearing with his son: "His father had never interfered with him by asking, 'Why do you behave as you do?'" (1 Kings 1:6). The word *interfere* in the Hebrew means "to displease or vex." Adonijah grew up self-centered and faithless, and he tried to usurp the throne (see 1 Kings 1–2).

Teaching boundaries is difficult! Most parents have a struggle maintaining boundaries and training their children to develop them. Below are a few obstacles you should be aware of.

Depending on the Child

"Why can't I spend the night with Madelaine?" whined thirteen-year-old Beverly to her mother, Samantha. Tentatively, Samantha said, "Honey, remember that you've already been out two nights this week, and it's a school night. I'm sure you can see Madelaine another time."

"You just don't want me to have friends! I never get to do anything I want, never, never!" With that pronouncement, Beverly stomped out of the kitchen and upstairs to her room.

Samantha then began the ancient dance she and her daughter had danced for many years. Samantha wanted and needed Beverly to be happy and close; their relationship was a central source of support for her. It was too painful for her to endure her daughter's distance. Standing outside the closed door to the bedroom, she said, "Maybe I've been a little harsh. You've had a tough week. I guess one more night won't hurt."

The door burst open, and Beverly embraced Samantha and exclaimed, "Mom, you're the best!" Samantha had once again reestablished contact with her daughter—and had unknowingly protected Beverly from the rigors of growing up.

There is no greater ingredient of growth for your youngster than love. As your child's major source, you provide the closeness, intimacy, and nurture that sustains her. Yet this closeness can become confused with a parent's need for the child. This is called dependency. It is the reverse of what the parenting relationship should be.

Most of us have a strong desire for family. We want a place to belong, where we are welcomed and understood. God created you with that desire and need. In fact, he "sets the lonely in families" (Psalm 68:6). We grow up, seek out a mate, and set up a nest. This is a good and necessary process. Being in a family meets many of our needs.

The problem arises, however, when parents need a child's closeness or affection to meet their own unmet needs. The child is unwittingly used to bring warmth, bonding, and love to the parent; this turns the child into a parent much too early in life. For example, one of my clients who came from a large family once asked his mother why she had had so many kids. "Because I never again want to be lonely like I was in my childhood," she replied.

Children will gladly enter the role of parent with Mom or Dad. It's not that they want this position; it's that they go where the relationship is. If soothing, comforting, and taking care of Dad's emotional needs gets them connected, they will take on that role.

Not only does this cause problems for children later in life, such as becoming a caretaker or becoming depressed or compulsive, but also a parent's dependency on a child can compromise the parent's ability to structure appropriate limits with the child. When you need someone's love, it is extremely difficult to confront or deprive him, as you risk losing this love via withdrawal, anger, or guilty feelings. As a result, the child isn't disciplined properly and learns the lesson that he can get what he wants if he pulls away the love. Though neither is aware of it, the child is emotionally blackmailing the parent. The parent tries to keep everything pleasant between them, so as not to cut off the flow of relationship.

Ask yourself a tough, honest question: *Am I afraid that if I say no to my kids, I will lose the love I need from them?* If that is the case, begin taking your needs for relationship to other places. These needs are good and God-given: It is not good for us to be alone (Genesis 2:18). But children have tough enough burdens to bear just growing up. Don't add yourself to them. Find friends, a church, and support groups that can help you satisfy your need to belong.

Overidentifying with the Child

Troy and his wife, Catherine, were excited. It had been a while since they had gone on a real, live date away from three-year-old Gavin. They had dinner and a concert planned. When the baby-sitter knocked at the door, Gavin shyly said hi to her. But when he saw Troy and Catherine putting on their coats, he started wailing and clinging to his mom's knees.

"C'mon, Cathy," Troy said, pulling her arm. "He'll be okay." But his wife felt paralyzed. As she looked at the tears brimming in her child's eyes, she experienced a deep sense of how abandoned and alone Gavin must feel right now. She felt his pain and anguish, seeing how little he was. And she knew she had to make a choice. "Can we reschedule, Honey?" she entreated Troy. "He would just be too upset and scared." Her husband sighed and took off his coat. Another date night flushed away.

Parents are commonly unable to delay their children's gratification because they overidentify with the child's feelings. Parents need to empathize with their children's pain, fear, and loneliness. In this way kids become filled up inside, their feelings are validated and understood, and they learn how to handle and use their emotions. However, some parents confuse their own painful feelings with their child's, thinking that the child is in more trouble than he actually is. Parents project their problems onto the child. What might be discomfort for the toddler is seen as trauma by the mother; what may be anxiety for the teen is experienced as panic by the father.

Often, this is a symptom of a parent's unworked-through issues. For example, Catherine had been emotionally abandoned by her own parents. They would withdraw love and pull away when she wasn't perfect, and they would not talk to her for long periods of time. After Catherine grew up and married, whenever Troy would get home late or go on a business trip, she would become uneasy and insecure, feeling unprotected and all alone. She would try to shake it off, but the feelings persisted. Her childhood abandonment emerged often in her marriage.

Catherine "read" her own feelings in Gavin when he protested her leaving. His cry pierced her heart, cutting all the way down to her own brokenness. The difference, however, was that Gavin had never been abandoned. Catherine's diligent and consistent affection had made her son into a very well-loved child. His tears were not the wounds of an unloved person, but the normal grief of a three-year-old who needs to learn to handle Mom's absences.

If you find that you can't bear your child's pain, you may be projecting your pain into him. Take a look at past issues that may not have healed. Seek wise counsel to investigate these problems. You need it, and your child needs a parent who can distinguish between *hurt* and *harm*.

Thinking Love and Separateness Are Enemies

When twelve-year-old Ron brought home a report card full of low grades, Susie told Keith, "It's time for some consequences. Ron has a high IQ, and the teachers say he just fools around during class. You and I need to talk about loss of phone, nights out, television, or whatever to fix this."

"Sweetheart, I know the grades are a problem," replied Keith. "But Ron needs to know we love him. If we put the hammer down like that, he'll think we don't care about him, and we could lose him to gangs. Let's just sit down and reason with him— I'm sure he'll come around."

As you can imagine, Ron didn't "come around" for a long time— not until he dropped out of vocational school four years later and joined the army. The structure in the army helped him grow up, but at what a loss of time and opportunity! Keith had made the common error of believing that structuring and being separate from his son were the same thing as a loss of love. He didn't want to do anything to jeopardize his friendship with his son.

Many parents misunderstand this issue. They fear that disagreeing, confronting, or simply being different from their children indicates a break in the connection. So they go along without comment until things really break down. The reality is that love and separateness go together and one doesn't threaten the other. *In fact, to the extent that you can be separate from someone is the extent to which you can truly love him or her.*

If you never disagree with the person you love, something is terribly wrong. Some people are afraid to be themselves with another person. Such fear negates love. The Bible says that "perfect love drives out fear" (1 John 4:18). You can't really love someone with whom you can't be separate. That is, love does not mean losing yourself, but rather frees you and empowers you to be yourself.

The most loving thing Keith could have done would have been to sit Ron down and spell out what his choices were going to cost him, so that he could begin to mature. He would have shown his son that they were two separate people who disagreed on how the boy was running his life. Yet he would have been showing Ron how deeply he cared for him and wanted the best for him.

When you keep set boundaries for your child, she actually feels more secure and loved, not less. She knows that you value her freedom to choose her path within certain parameters and that you will guard and develop this freedom with her.

You may feel that when you tell the truth to your child, love is gone. You may feel that when you are close to your child, you can't be honest. If this is true, begin to work on being a truthful, honest person with both God and the supportive people in your life. The good people will draw closer and love you more. The bad ones will very likely just go away. Remember that in God's character, love and truth are friends: "Righteousness [*truthfulness*] and peace [*love*] kiss each other" (Psalm 85:10).

Ignoring and Zapping

Carol considered patience one of her virtues. She was able to smooth others' problems, see the "big picture," and wait for change and results. This virtue was often tested in her parenting of five-year-old Tess, who was endowed with a very strong will. In the grocery store Tess would loudly and repeatedly demand toys and ice cream. Carol thought it best to ignore the behavior, hoping that it would go away. It didn't. Each trip to the market brought louder and more embarrassing demands from Tess.

Finally, a friend of hers happened to be shopping at the same time as Carol and Tess. "My, your daughter certainly knows how to get her way," the friend said.

Carol was mortified. When they got into the car, Tess again demanded a cookie. Carol lit into her daughter: "Young lady, you've pushed me too far! You've pushed and you've pushed and you've pushed, and I've had it up to here with your behavior in the store! You're going straight to your room when we get home, and just wait till your father hears about this!" Whatever patience Carol possessed had vanished, as she ranted and raved. Tess was horrified, and she cried all the way home. Carol felt both guilty and powerless.

Unknowingly, Carol was taking what we call the "ignore and zap" approach with Tess. She was putting up with inappropriateness, hoping it would go away. Instead, it escalated. At the same time, her resentment was growing. Finally, all the truths she had neglected to say boiled out at one time, and Tess felt hurt and frightened. This common inconsistency is rooted in a belief that bad things will simply work themselves out. Unfortunately, that's not the way the world works. You don't treat infections that way, or holes in the roof of your house. Generally, problems not dealt with get worse over time, not better.

Children are the same way. They don't have internal brakes on their demanding or inappropriate behaviors: "Folly is bound up in the heart of a child" (Proverbs 22:15). They need their parents to be their external boundary, correcting, limiting, and providing consequences, until boundaries that were external become internal. This is why consistency in confronting problem behaviors early in the game is so important.

Ignoring and zapping teaches the child she should persist in whatever she wants. She learns she can get away with murder nine times out of ten, and she just needs to learn how to endure the out-of-control parent that one time out of ten. Those are excellent odds. You would probably be eager to invest in a stock that had a ninety percent chance of success. To avoid teaching this lesson, become an early confronter, and ask your friends to help you be consistent with your parenting. It helps you to prepare your child for real life, in which she will not get everything she wants, no matter how much she tries.

Being Worn Down

It is scary how our kids can sense when we are weak and ready to give in to them. Many a parent can identify with the smart adolescent who begs, pleads, argues, and rationalizes for hours to get out of some responsibility. A couple of friends of mine said their son regularly argued for forty-five minutes about taking out the trash—a ten-minute job! He didn't mind losing the time as long as he didn't have to do the task.

Kids work us and work us and work us. They don't give up easily. And the later you start serious boundary training, the more energetically your children will resist. It's hard to give up playing God when you've been doing it a long time. We empathize with parents who figure, "Oh well, I'll give in this time and give them the money. It's just not worth the fight." And that may be true on some occasions. But each time you let them neglect responsibilities, the child's ability to be a self-controlled person is eroded.

If you notice your child wearing you down, it might mean a couple of things. First, you may be in a state of deprivation, either because you are isolated from supportive relationships or you lack time to yourself. We can't keep boundaries in a vacuum. Get into regular, helpful relationships, or arrange for some time to yourself to fill up your tank. Remember that parenting is a temporary job, not an identity. Kids with parents who have a life learn both that they aren't the center of the universe and that they can be free to pursue their own dreams.

Second, you may have trained your child to go just so far and you'll give in. As a good friend told me, "The trick of parenting is to hold onto your limit one more time than your children hold onto the demand. That's all you need—one more." You need cheerleader friends who will help you hold that line a couple of thousand times. The good news is, as you do, children understand that Mom really does mean it this time, and they begin to deescalate their efforts.

Remember, you can't train what you don't have. Don't just *say* boundaries to your child. *Be* boundaries. If you aren't yet, get to work on yourself. It will pay off for both you and him.

We hope you are now motivated and encouraged by the importance of training your children in boundaries and of being a parent with boundaries. In the next section you will gain an understanding of the ten laws of boundaries. These guiding principles will help you apply boundaries to many aspects of home life with your kids. Use them as tools with your children to employ and teach responsibility.

Part 2

————

Ten Boundary Principles
Kids Need to Know

— 4 —

What Will Happen If I Do This?

The Law of Sowing and Reaping

S ally had big plans for the family. They were going to Disneyland, and she relished the idea of the fun they were going to have. Planning to leave at noon, she began at breakfast to think of what everyone needed to do before they left. She wanted her son Jason to do some yard work he had been putting off—a common occurrence—because they had to return some rakes and things to a friend that day.

Sally told Jason that he "must" do the work before they left. She emphasized how it had to "absolutely" be done before 11:30 A.M., so he needed to make sure he started soon. An hour later he had not started, and she reminded him again. Thirty minutes after that, she repeated the reminder.

She got busy with some other things and at 11:30 walked into the den, only to find Jason watching television.

"What are you doing?" she screamed. "I told you to get the yard done before we left. Now we are all going to be late! I cannot believe that you have done this to us."

She continued complaining angrily until she, Dad, one sister, and Jason had all chipped in to get the yard work done so that they could finally leave at 1:10 P.M. The ride to Disneyland was less than amiable, filled with quiet scorn for Jason. The rest of the day was affected as well.

Down the street, a similar scenario had occurred with different results. Susan had plans to go shopping for the afternoon with her three daughters. She had given them all instructions about what they needed to get done before they left. She told them that they would leave at one o'clock, and those who didn't have their jobs done wouldn't go.

About fifteen minutes before departure time she found that Jen, the middle one, had not finished her chores.

"Looks like you have chosen not to go," Susan said to Jen. "That's sad. We'll miss you."

"You can't do that to me. That's not fair!" Jen exclaimed.

"I think I was pretty clear that the jobs needed to be done before we went shopping. I am really sad that you chose not to do them. We'll see you later. By the way, I don't really have time now to figure out a consequence for not getting them done by dinner, but maybe we won't have to worry about that. I hope you choose to avoid another penalty. We'll miss you. 'Bye."

Susan and her other two daughters had a wonderful afternoon.

Teaching the Reality Principle

Parents run into a big problem when they do not distinguish between psychological and negative relational consequences versus reality consequences. Life works on *reality consequences*. Psychological and negative *relational consequences*, such as getting angry, sending guilt messages, nagging, and withdrawing love, usually do not motivate people to change. If they do, the change is short-lived, directed only at getting the person to lighten up on the psychological pressure. True change usually comes only when someone's behavior causes him to encounter *reality consequences* like pain or losses of time, money, possessions, things he enjoys, and people he values.

In the above scenarios, Sally and Susan had basically the same situation, but their responses were the opposite. Sally used psychological and negative relational consequences and prevented reality consequences. Susan avoided psychological consequences and used reality consequences.

In short, Susan was letting Jen experience the Law of Sowing and Reaping. She sowed irresponsibility and reaped the consequence: the loss of something she valued. Isn't that the way the real world works? Isn't an understanding of that law something she will need as an adult? Consider what God says: "A man

Sally's Consequences for Jason	Susan's Consequences for Jen
• Nagging through the morning so that Jason didn't have to watch the time.	• No nagging along the way. She assumed that Jen could read a clock if she wanted to.
• Screaming and displays of anger that got the attention off the real problem—lateness—and turned Sally into the real problem for Jason. For example, instead of "I am late and in danger of missing something," the problem became "I have a crazy mother."	• No emotional reactions that would make her a problem for Jen.
• Taking the victim stance to the child's behavior—"We are going to be late. Look what you've done"—thus teaching the child that he is in control of the whole family's day and mood.	• Not being victimized by the behavior of the child. She stayed in control of her own life, not letting Jen's behavior derail the family's plan or mood.
• Stirring up all the wrong emotions in the child (guilt, resentment, and anger) instead of the only one that helps him change—sadness.	• Stirring up no emotional reactions in Jen and thus letting Jen be free to experience her own loss.
• Worst of all, making sure that the behavior did not cost the child anything but grief from Mom, toward which he has long since become deaf.	• Making sure the behavior cost the child the opportunity to do something that she valued.

reaps what he sows. The one who sows to please his sinful nature, from that nature will reap destruction; the one who sows to please the Spirit, from the Spirit will reap eternal life" (Galatians 6:7-8).

And isn't it true that when we are allowed to pay for our mistakes, we learn from them? Reality losses cause us to change our behavior.

The Law of Sowing and Reaping is a law that we depend on daily, both positively and negatively. God has wired it into the universe, and we can build a life around it. On the positive side, we depend on it to have good things happen:

- If I work hard, I can advance in my career.
- If I make enough calls, I will make some sales.
- If I study my Bible and seek God, I will grow spiritually in my relationship with him.
- If I spend time being open with the people I care about, my relationships will grow.

Or bad things:

- If I eat everything I want, I will gain weight or develop heart disease.
- If I yell at the ones I care about, I will hurt them and cause distance between us.
- If I don't push myself to grow vocationally, I will stay stuck at a level that ultimately will not fulfill me.
- If I don't watch my spending, I can get into financial bondage and lose my freedom.

The positive side of the Law of Sowing and Reaping gives us a reasonable sense of power and control over our lives. This is what God intended, and he is pleased when we invest our talents and lives to reap good fruit (Matthew 25:14–30). Both the Bible and life experience show that effort, diligence, and responsibility pay off.

The negative side of the Law of Sowing and Reaping gives us a healthy fear of bad things. A healthy respect for consequences keeps us living in reality and moving in a good direction. Through the consequences of relational failures, for example, we learn to love in a way that succeeds.

But if we never learn the Law of Sowing and Reaping, we lose on both the positive and negative sides of life. We do not have the motivation to do good work and be diligent, and at the same time we do not fear laziness, irresponsibility, and other character problems. Both conditions result in suffering: the loss of good realities and the encountering of bad ones.

Think of what Jason was learning: You do not have to do your part, for everyone will do it for you. Bad things will not happen when you don't perform. You can blow off your responsibilities and still go to Disneyland. You don't lose anything. Sure, people yell at you, but if you tune them out, yelling will not be a problem. It will be good practice later with bosses and spouses.

Too Bad for Whom?

Consequences transfer the need to be responsible from the parent to the child. Consequences make it *the child's problem.*

I was at a friend's house one day when I asked their nine-year-old son to go outside and shoot some baskets with me.

"I can't. I have to stay inside," he said.

"How come?"

"My mom was talking on the phone, and I kept interrupting her. Too bad for me."

"Too bad for me." This is the lesson consequences teach a child. "My behavior becomes a problem for *me.*" Too many times, children's behavior does not become a problem for them. It does not cost them things they value.

Instead, parents allow the problem to become a problem for them instead of their children. Remember, the child needs to worry about and solve the problem. So the role of the parent is to help the child want to do that. Consequences provide this motivation.

Jen learned that her lateness was her problem and not her mother's. You can bet that the next time she was told that she would miss something if she were not finished with a task by a certain time, she watched the clock. But Jason has not yet learned that his behavior is *his* problem. It is still his mother's problem. She had the worry, strain, and effort. He still got to go on the trip.

In parenting situations, remember these few questions when figuring out what to do:

1. Whose problem is this?
2. What can I do to help him experience the problem?
3. What am I doing to keep him from experiencing the problem?

Age and Content Change, the Law Remains the Same

The Law of Sowing and Reaping teaches children "self-control" (Galatians 5:23)—one of the most basic lessons in life. They learn, "I am in control of the quality of my life." They realize that they have a choice whether they are inside and miserable or outside and playing. Choose to do your chores, you play. Choose to avoid your chores, you pay. Either way, you are in control of your life, not your parents.

When a child is a toddler, the content may be "Don't touch, or you have to sit in the time-out chair." As a young child, it may be "Don't ride your bike past the corner, or you lose it." As a teenager, it may be "Don't get a speeding ticket, or you lose use of the car." Of course, the opposite happens as they exercise good choices. "Since you are not breaking the rules, you can play there as long as you like." "Since you have stayed in the limits so well and are so careful, let's talk about riding further." "Your driving record is so good, I am willing to talk about letting you drive to that concert in San Diego now."

The particulars will always change, depending on the context in which the child—and later the adult—finds herself. If she doesn't throw food, she can eat at the table. If she sells her quota, she can manage an entire region. The content is different, but the law is the same. If I make good choices, life is better than if I don't.

The formula for this is to give children freedom, allow choices, and then manage the consequences accordingly. Heap on the praise and increase the freedoms when children use responsibility well. Make sure they know why they are getting more privileges—because of their trustworthiness.

When children make bad choices, empathize with their loss. Avoid the "I told you so's." Empathy sounds like this:

- "That's sad not getting to play today."
- "I know. I feel for you missing the game. I hate it when I don't get to do something I want."
- "I bet you are hungry. I hate to miss a meal too."

Compare the above statements with the following:

- "Don't come crying to me. If you had just done your work you wouldn't be in this mess."
- "Don't give me the 'It's not fair' thing. You made your bed, now you have to lie in it."
- "Well, if you would have done your chores and behaved, you would have gotten to eat with us. But maybe next time you won't be so selfish and place all of us in jeopardy of eating late."

Children could easily resent a person saying this second set of statements. They then would focus more on hating the parent who is making them feel bad than on correcting the behavior that got them into this mess. We can't overemphasize the role of empathy for the child who makes a bad choice. It builds a bridge to you instead of a barrier.

Balancing Freedom, Choices, and Consequences

The goal is not to control the children to make them do what you want. The goal is to give them the choice to do what they want, and make it so painful to do the wrong thing that they will not want to. Who wants to be grounded all day? This way, you are not making them do anything. You are letting them choose, but making the Law of Sowing and Reaping have reality. If they sow to irresponsibility, they will reap pain. And if they sow to responsible behavior, they will reap the benefits and want to choose that path.

Little Joey wants two incompatible things:

1. He wants to do things his way.
2. He wants things to go well for him.

Joey's mother also wants two things:

1. She wants things to go well for Joey.
2. She wants Joey to do the right thing.

Mom knows what Joey needs to do to grow up into a responsible adult, and she is in control of dishing out the privileges, freedoms, rewards, and punishments Joey needs to make his life go well. *If she can just remember that her job is to make sure that Joey does not get both his wishes, she is doing well.* He can have one of them, but not both. If he chooses to do things his way, things will likely not go well for him. If things go well for him, it is often because he has chosen well. Parents are in control of the reaping.

In addition, no adult can have these two things: "I want to be successful," and "I want to do whatever I want every day." Adults must choose one or the other, and so must children.

The key here is that the child has to have the choice of one or the other. That is the essence of freedom and the root of self-control. Self-control doesn't exist without freedom and choices. So the parent's task is to give the proper amount of freedom and choices and then manage the consequences. Remember a basic theological truth:

Freedom = Responsibility = Consequences = Love

To the extent that all these are equal, we are doing well. If our child is free to choose and held responsible for the consequences of his actions, we will develop a loving person who is doing the right thing for the right reasons. If any one of these is out of balance—for example, more freedom granted than someone is held responsible for—then character problems grow. Or if someone is held responsible but is not free to choose, she is a slave and a robot, and she will not choose lovingly, but only out of compliance and resentment. Or if someone is free and responsible for something but does not suffer the consequences of misusing his freedom, then he develops character problems and ends up doing very irresponsible and unloving things.

A child has small amounts of freedom, choices in that freedom, and consequences in those choices, and develops love as a result. And it is no different for an adult. Give freedom, require responsibility, render consequences, and be loving throughout.

Running Interference

Parents have difficulty allowing their children to suffer consequences. The natural tendency is to bail them out. Here is a test for you: How many late nights have you spent helping with a school project that was due the next morning, but was also sprung on you the night before? The scene usually goes like this:

"Mom, I need some glue for my project."

"Sorry, dear. We don't have any."

"But I have to have it. The project is due tomorrow."

"When did you know about this assignment?"

"Two weeks ago."

"Why didn't you get the glue before now?"

"I forgot."

"The nearest store open this late is twenty minutes away. How could you do this to me?"

"I'm sorry, Mom. But I have to have it done, or I will get a bad grade."

"Okay, get in the car."

(Sometimes Mom is frustrated and angry, but sometimes Mom might not mind at all.)

Compare this with the Mom who has an eye on the future:

"Mom, I need some glue for my project."

"Sorry, dear, I don't have any."

"But I have to have it. The project's due tomorrow."

"What teacher would call and give you an assignment at this hour without enough time to get the supplies?"

"Come on, Mom. She gave it to us at school."

"When?"

"Two weeks ago."

"Oh. So you have had two weeks to get glue and your other supplies?"

"Yes, but I thought we had them."

"Oh. That's sad. Seems like I remember this happening with the felt you needed for your last project. Well, I don't have any, and it is past my bedtime. So I hope you can figure out something to make that does not require glue. Good night, honey. I'm pulling for you."

Mom number two looked into the future to see what character lesson she could teach her child today that would ensure a better future for him. She saw a pattern developing. This was not the first time her son had made a last-minute request for material. We would not have a problem with a mom helping out in a pinch with a child who normally thinks ahead, plans responsibly, and gets assignments done on time. But Mom number two was not dealing with a child like that. She saw a character pattern developing that would make life difficult for her child:

- Last minute attempts to get projects done for a boss and losing jobs
- Getting in trouble with the IRS for not having taxes done or information intact
- Destroying relationships because of the tendency to not pull one's weight and depending on others to always be responsible

So she decided not to interfere with the Law of Sowing and Reaping and allowed the law to do its work. The child sowed to procrastination and would have to pay the penalty for his lack of planning. The consequences would teach him a lesson far more cheaply than learning it later in life. Whatever school privilege he was going to lose was a lot less than the adult version resulting from the same behavior.

The law works—if we don't get in the way. But too often we do. We run interference by interrupting the consequences before they can teach our children the lesson they were designed to teach. Too often children don't learn until later in life, when no one will bail them out. The addiction or pattern of irresponsibility has taken its toll on everyone around them, and these people are sick of it. It is the parents' job to get sick of bailing a child out now instead of others getting sick of it later—and then to cure their own "sick of it" feeling by not bailing the child out anymore.

To do this, parents need to be comfortable with letting the child suffer. As the Bible says, "No discipline seems pleasant at the time, but painful. Later on, however, it produces a harvest of righteousness and peace for those who have been trained by it" (Hebrews 12:11). The Greek word for "painful" is a word that means "a grievous, grudging, heavy sorrow." That is not pretty. But to get to the fruit of discipline, there has to be pain. Parents often resist allowing the consequences of the Law of Sowing and Reaping because they overidentify with the child's pain. Let children suffer the sorrow now instead of later. Suffering is inevitable. Make sure it happens when the consequences of irresponsibility are a loss of privileges, not the loss of a career or a marriage.

If you find it difficult to allow your child to suffer consequences, be sure to find someone to help you through your own resistance. You may be dealing with your own hurt from the past, your own lack of boundaries, or codependent patterns learned in childhood. Getting support from a good counselor or parent support group may be essential to taking the stance your child needs.

Balancing Grace and Truth

We have often talked about how grace and truth must be balanced for growth to occur, and we shall say more about this later. But in short, the recipe for a growing person is always grace plus truth over time. Give a person grace (unmerited favor) and truth (structure), and do that over time, and you have the greatest chance of this person growing into a person of good character.

Grace includes support, resources, love, compassion, forgiveness, and all of the relational sides of God's nature. Truth is the structure of life; it tells us how we are supposed to live our lives and how life really works. The Law of Sowing and Reaping is basic to successful living. Parents can tell children over and over what is good for them; they can preach about the way things ought to be and the way to success and a good life. But until their teaching and preaching becomes true for the child in his experience of consequences, it is only theory, nagging, and parental noise. For the truth to be true to a child or anyone else, it has to be real, not just a concept. If Mom tells me it's good for me to do *a, b,* or *c,* then I need for that to be reality for me to learn it. It is her job to make it real. Then and only then is the truth *really* true.

Making Good the Law of Sowing and Reaping

The list of reality consequences is endless. The only end is your own creativity. But here are some suggestions.

- Make the consequences a natural outflow of the crime. For example, if I am late getting ready for a movie, I may not get to go. If I am perpetually late getting to dinner, I may miss eating. If I'm late preparing for my project, I may get a bad grade. If I don't do my chores around the house, I may lose a privilege the rest of the family enjoys. If I don't tell my parents where I'm going, I may stay home next time.
- Save consequences for serious offenses. In general, the consequences we have been discussing are for behavior that is in danger of becoming a bad character pattern. All of us need flexibility and understanding at times. All employers, for example, post sick-leave policies. Schools excuse absences for a good reason. But if someone has an excuse for everything, it's no longer an excuse, but a rationalization. We get to the consequences stage when reasoning, warnings, and talking have failed.
- Give immediate consequences. The younger the child, the more immediate the consequence needs to be. With very young children, firm nos, time-outs, isolation, a swat on the behind, and removal from the situation work well.

- Stay away from emotional consequences, and effect reality consequences. Anger, guilt, and shame do not teach Johnny to do better. Feeling the pain of loss of TV privileges, money, or computer time teaches him much better.
- Use relational consequences only if they concern your own feelings. If Jill's behavior is hurting you or others, tell her so and say what you plan to do about your feelings. "It saddens me when you talk to me that way. I don't like to be spoken to like that; it makes me feel far away from you. So I won't be listening when you are sassing or disrespectful. I don't allow myself to listen to talk like that. When you want to talk differently, I will be glad to listen."
- Think of consequences as protecting yourself and the rest of the family from the behavior of the child. *In other words, your own boundaries are the best boundaries.* "I do not like to eat with people bickering. Jimmy, go to your room, and when you can stop bickering, you can return to dinner. By the way, I clear the table at 7:30, and there is no more food after that. Later snacks are only for those who ate dinner." Or, "We like to be able to use the community areas like the den for the family's space. We don't like to trip over your stuff there. I will impound any toys that are still out when I go to bed because we don't like a messy family room. You will have to pay to get them back."

A friend's daughter would not respect her wishes to end some conversations and endless questioning sessions. To her daughter, Susie, she would say, "Talking time is over."

"But I'm not through talking," her daughter would reply.

Her answer was perfect: "I know, Susie. That's okay. But I'm through listening."

Your own boundaries are the best boundaries.

- Preserve choice as much as possible. In situations where only one option is available to the child, like leaving to go with the family, still give a choice. "You can go and have fun with us, or you can go and not try. Which would you like? And by the way, if you are a pain for us to be around, we'll have to remember that when it is time to go to the movies."

- Make sure there is not a good reason a child is misbehaving before invoking consequences. Check for fears and medical or emotional problems. A child may be acting out pain, hurt feelings, powerlessness, or some other emotional state that needs to be connected with. For example, it is not unusual for children to begin to act out or regress when something is going on within the family, such as a divorce, marital stress, or a move. The pain could be in direct response to being hurt by a parent or another child. Children can hurt in myriad ways, and often their misbehavior is a sign of pain that needs more than limits. See the chapter on empathy.

- Talk to the child and ask about the misbehavior. Do this at a time when the child is not misbehaving. "When you do such and such, I would like to understand why you do that. Is there something you are trying to tell me? Are you angry with me, or hurt about something? What do you think would be a good plan for us the next time that happens?"

A Further Word on Rewards and Consequences

A mom told me recently that she had told her son to do something minimal like take out the trash, and his reply was "What will you give me?" She asked me what a good reward would be. I told her to tell him that she would give him a very hard time if he didn't do what she asked. She looked at me funny, but we had an interesting discussion about rewards and punishment.

We believe in rewards for these two things:

1. Acquiring new skills
2. Performing exceptionally

We do not believe in rewards for these:

1. Doing the age-appropriate requirements of civilized people (such as living skills)
2. Doing what is expected (such as work)

Rewards such as praise, snacks, money, a trip to the zoo, or stars on the fridge can be powerful teachers of new skills. Sometimes when we are learning something new that takes a lot of effort, we need the motivation of short-term gratification of rewards along the way. Children love a reward for learning something new.

Rewards can be good also when someone surpasses what is normally expected. Schools recognize this kind of performance, as do scouts, athletic organizations, and employers. Incentive performance and various perks are a big part of motivating employees.

Certain normal behavior is expected from a civilized human being. Cities, landlords, employers, schools, friends, spouses all expect a certain level of performance from an adult with whom they are in relationship. Once children have learned the skills required for responsible living, these should be expected without reward. To the contrary, it should cost them if they do not do them.

We reward a two-year-old for learning potty training, not an adult for being able to continue it. You did not get a reward last week for getting to work on time. It was expected. But if you were late more than a few times, you would probably get docked or disciplined in some way.

Be careful of giving children the attitude that they only have to perform when someone pays them for it. They need to learn that they will have to pay if they don't perform. This avoids the attitude of "entitlement," the feeling that many people have today that they are entitled to something for nothing. It is better for them to learn that everyone in the family is required to do one's part. If you do more than your part, we can talk about some extra reward, but we expect the minimum from everyone. As Jesus said, "Would he thank the servant because he did what he was told to do?" (Luke 17:9). In the real world, no award dinners are held for minimum performance. But many penalties are dealt out for failure to meet minimum civilized expectations.

Reality As Friend

Maturity is when we stop demanding that life meet our demands and begin to meet the demands of life. The Law of Sowing and Reaping forces us meet the demands of life, or we experience pain. We change our behavior when the pain of staying the same becomes greater than the pain of changing. Consequences give us the pain that motivates us to change.

Reality is not our enemy, but our friend. Doing things in the way that reality demands has great rewards: "My son, do not forget my teaching, but keep my commands in your heart, for they will prolong your life many years and bring you prosperity. Let love and faithfulness never leave you. . . . Then you will win favor and a good name in the sight of God and man" (Proverbs 3:1–4). A mature person knows that the good way is the best way. To live wisely, to make good choices, to do the right thing is to have a good life.

In the mind of a child, however, reality is the enemy. Consequences teach children that reality can indeed be their friend. To make the necessary changes in behavior and meet the demands of reality can mean that things go better. We learn that we are ultimately in control of much of how our life goes. If we sow to meeting reality's demands, we reap the benefits. If we sow to avoiding reality, reality will ultimately demand that we pay up. And in the end, that is not friendly.

Do your children a favor and teach them to make friends with reality early in life. It is cheaper and safer, and your dinners will begin on time.

But to do that, they must learn to be responsible for the right things. In the next chapter, we will show you what those are.

— 5 —

Pulling My Own Wagon

The Law of Responsibility

When my (Dr. Townsend's) sons, Ricky and Benny, were younger, they argued a lot, as siblings do. My wife, Barbi, and I often functioned as moderator and judge for them. One of us would sit at the kitchen table, and they would each present their complaints about the other's horrible maltreatment. We got the facts as best we could, decided who was right and wrong, and suggested how to fix the problem: Return the toy, apologize, or whatever.

This system of arbitration worked fine until I noticed that we were spending more and more time doing it. Every time I sat down to read the paper or talk to my wife, I'd have to drop it all and play judge. The boys depended more and more on our flawed wisdom. Finally, I had an idea.

"Let's change this deal," I told them. "From now on, nobody comes to me or Mom unless you've already spent some time working it out between you. Try to fix the problem. Then, if it isn't better, you can come to us. But if you do come to us, the person who was wrong will probably suffer a consequence."

It took a while, but the boys began doing this. They had two incentives. First, the culprit, who wanted to get the issue resolved without a parental consequence, was eager to negotiate! Second, they took pride in not needing their parents for resolving little squabbles.

In fact, I had to deal with my own codependence one day when I saw them arguing. Wanting to be helpful, I walked up and said, "Okay, what's going on, guys?"

Benny turned to me impatiently and said, "Dad, we're working it out."

Chastened, I slunk back to my chair. I wasn't needed right then.

The boys were learning a valuable boundary lesson: They are responsible for themselves and their struggles. *Children need to know that their problems are their own problems, no one else's.* Their life is their own little red wagon, and their job is to pull it, without expecting someone else to. The corollary to this is that while children should care about their relationships, they should not take on others' problems. They are responsible *for* themselves and *to* others. (See more on this below, under "Loving Vs. Rescuing.")

One of the hallmarks of maturity is taking responsibility for one's own life, desires, and problems. If we show up late for work, we don't blame the freeway. If we want to advance our career, we take courses. If we are angry, we deal with whatever made us angry rather than waiting for someone to soothe our feelings. Mature adults see themselves as problem solvers instead of trying to find someone else to blame or to solve problems for them.

Immature people experience life as victims and constantly want someone else to solve their problems. One definition of an addict, for example, is a person who has someone else paying his debts. Yet, as the Bible teaches, "each one should carry his own load" (Galatians 6:5).

Taking responsibility for themselves does not come naturally to children. During the first year of life, the infant is busy with the opposite task—learning to depend and need. She is working on taking in love and comfort from Mother and learning to trust. Her life is truly in someone else's hands, and she can perish without the right kind of attentiveness. Yet, even then, she is learning to take responsibility for her own part in getting her needs met. She cries when she is distressed, alerting Mother that something is wrong. She holds out her arms to be held. She pushes away when she wants to be put down. God has constructed us so that even from the beginning we are learning to shoulder our own load in life.

So a large part of your boundary training with your kids will have to do with helping them understand that they must gradually take responsibility for their own problems. *What begins as the parent's burden must end up as the child's.*

These are difficult words for many people, especially adults who have been hurt emotionally in their own childhood. They didn't get something they needed, like caring, security, or structure. Or they got some things they didn't need, like rage, distance, or overcriticism. And they themselves have to repair what was broken, rather than whoever caused the problem. And it is not fair.

But since the Fall in the Garden of Eden, things haven't been fair. Bad things happen to good people. But if we wait for justice, we are putting our lives under the control of those who hurt us. Better far to take God's solution of grief and forgiveness and grow through the unfair situation. Remember that God himself didn't demand fairness and justice for us; rather, he valued his relationship with us so much that he went to the cross for us: "Christ died for the ungodly" (Romans 5:6).

At one of our seminars, someone in the audience asked, "How much of who I am today is my responsibility, and how much is the result of my environment?" In other words, the questioner wanted to know how much his parents' treatment of him had influenced him.

For grins, Henry and I each wrote down on a separate piece of paper what percentage of responsibility for one's life we thought the child bears and what percentage the parents bear. When we put our papers together, they had the exact same numbers: We felt that the child bears seventy percent of the responsibility, and the parent, thirty percent.

Now, these percentages aren't etched in stone. But it reflects our own conclusions that, even though we all have been sinned against and mistreated in some ways, our own responses to our environments are the major determining forces in our present character and personality. The child bears most of the weight of his own development.

What Kids Need to Take Responsibility For

The aspects of life for which your kids need to take responsibility we call their *treasures*, or things of great value. Jesus taught that the kingdom of heaven is like treasure in a field, which is worth selling all we own to possess (Matthew 13:44). Part of that treasure is our character—how we love, work, and serve. We are to protect, develop, and mature our character, to grow not only in this life, but also in the next. Let's look at some of the treasures for which your child needs to take ownership.

Emotions

Cheryl was at the end of her rope. Eleven-year-old Nathan threw tantrums when he was frustrated. Tantrums at that age could be scary. He would yell at her, stomp, slam doors, and sometimes throw things. Yet Cheryl thought, *He needs a place to let out those bottled-up feelings, or they'll eat him up inside.* So she would let Nathan "express himself," or she would try to soothe and calm him. But his behavior escalated over time. Finally, a friend told her, "You're training him to be a male rage-aholic." Stunned, she got some advice.

With a little help, Cheryl changed her approach to Nathan's rage attacks. She told him, "I know things make you angry, and I feel for your frustration. Things do get to all of us. But your feelings are disturbing me and the rest of the family. So here's what we've come up with. When you're mad, you can tell us you're angry. We want you to be honest with your feelings. And if it's about us, we will sit down and try to resolve the problem. But yelling, cursing, stomping, and throwing aren't acceptable. If those happen, you'll need to go to your room without phone, computer, or music until you can be civil. Then, for the minutes that you've disrupted the family, you'll need to do that many extra minutes of housework. I hope we can help you with these feelings."

Nathan didn't believe Cheryl at first, but she stuck to her guns. He escalated his disruptive behavior for a while (parents, expect escalation; kids need to make sure you're serious), but Cheryl followed through with the consequences. She was tremendously anxious about this part, as she feared that Nathan would no longer have an outlet for his feelings. Would he blow up even more intensely? Would his spirit be quenched or broken?

Neither actually happened. After his initial period of protest, Nathan settled down. His tantrums became less intense and further apart. He began to bring his problems to Cheryl as problems, not as crises, and to work them out with her. What was happening inside Nathan is that he was becoming the master of his emotions. He was using feelings in the ways for which God created them: as signals about the state of our soul. He could be angry, but instead of having the emotion carry him out of control, he would identify the source of anger and solve whatever problem in life had led up to it. Nathan was beginning to own one of his treasures: his feelings.

Attitudes

Attitudes differ from feelings. Attitudes are the stances or opinions we take toward people and issues. For example, a person may have certain attitudes about how one gets along in life. A self-centered attitude would be, "I should get what I want in life by virtue of being me." A more mature one would be, "I will probably get what I work hard for in life." Attitudes are the basis for many of the major decisions we will make in a lifetime, involving love, marriage, career, and spirituality. Here is a brief list of the things about which your children need to cultivate an attitude:

- Self (strengths and weaknesses, likes and dislikes)
- Family role
- Friends
- God (who he is and how to relate to him)
- School (their interests and duties)
- Work
- Moral issues (sex, drugs, gangs)

To own their attitudes, children need help in two ways. They need to see that attitudes are something they work out and decide for themselves and that others' attitudes may not be the same as theirs. And we need to help them see the consequences of their attitudes, how they need to take responsibility for them.

Your child's attitude toward her family, for example, may be that "the family exists to meet my needs" rather than "I'm on a team in which everybody's needs are as important as mine." Show her how her attitude hurts her and others. Teach her the value of being in community and how her needs can be met there. And follow up your teaching with experiences that help her see these realities. For example, you may say, "Molly, if you can't wait for your brother to finish talking before you interrupt him, you'll have to wait until tomorrow to talk about your day. We really want to hear how school went, but you'll need to wait your turn." This helps develop an attitude of respect for others' feelings.

You will do your kids immeasurable favors by helping them experience the reality of Jesus' Log and Speck principle: Before you look at your friend's speck, take the log out of your own eye (Matthew 7:1–5 NASB). In other words, *teach your kids, whenever they have a problem, first to examine what they may have done to contribute to the problem.* Attitude has everything in the world to do with this issue. Here are some examples:

Situation	Speck	Log
A friend at school is mean to me.	She's so hateful.	How might I have hurt her?
I got a bad report card.	The teacher is weird.	How were my study habits?
I didn't get my full allowance.	My parents are unfair.	Which tasks did I not do?
My big brother beat me up.	I have a bad brother.	Am I provoking him and then crying victim?

Behavior

Children learn to conduct themselves in private and in public through love, teaching, modeling, and experiences. They need to learn that how they act is their responsibility.

By nature, kids are "impulse disorders." That is, they link their emotions to their actions with no intervening agents such as thoughts, values, or empathy for others. There is a direct line between their feelings and behavior. If this continues into adult life, they can become addicts or suffer character disorders. They simply discharge their feelings into their behavior. They have no sense of "What might happen if I act on my feelings?" Here is how the child (or the adult who has never learned boundaries) operates:

> Cause: I'm angry that you won't let me watch more TV.
>
> Effect: I whine and have a tantrum, and everything blows up.

The child with boundaries operates this way:

> Cause: I'm angry that you won't let me watch more TV.
>
> Thought: I could have a tantrum, but I could lose a lot more than TV. Better to submit.
>
> Effect: I'll go start doing my homework.

Your child doesn't come prepackaged with that intervening agent. However, God gave you, the parent, the tools to help build it into him, even without his cooperation. You simply make it more painful to be impulsive than to restrain his behavior. Many parents underestimate how much control children can exert over their own behavior (see the section on age-appropriate limits in chapter 3). Normal, healthy children with minds and wills of their own can learn to take ownership of their behavior.

You build intervening agents into children by validation, instruction, and experience. *Validation:* Let them know their feelings are real and authentic, whether or not they are realistic. *Instruction:* Tell them that acting on their anger or desire isn't appropriate. Give them ways to deal with their feelings, such as talking or substituting how you get what you need (for example, you get more privileges when respectful than when demanding). *Experience*: Give them consequences for the behavior if it's still inappropriate, and praise them when they take more ownership of their behavior.

For example, in one family I know, two sisters had a problem. The more verbally outgoing Taylor kept interrupting the quieter Heather. The parents sat down and said, "Taylor, we know you're excited about all you have to tell us [*validation*]. But it's rude to Heather and hurts her feelings when you interrupt her all the time. We would like for you to hold your thought until she's through talking. If you can't, we'll double the time Heather can talk until you can restrain yourself. We hope this helps you get more self-control, because otherwise this habit could make people resent you [*instruction*]."

Taylor listened and then tested the system, as is the child's job. Her parents held to it, and Taylor was very sad that on a couple of evenings Mom and Dad didn't really get to hear what happened to her at school [*experience*]. Then, Taylor's mother reported to me, something funny happened.

"The third night," she said, "Heather was talking, and I could see Taylor's face become more animated, as she had just thought of something important to tell us. She took a breath and opened her mouth. Heather even stopped talking in midsentence. Then, in the silence around the dinner table, Taylor's face changed. We could actually see her remembering all her lost opportunities in the previous two nights. And she looked at all of us, grinned, and said, 'What were you saying, Heather?' We nearly fell out of our chairs laughing."

Hooray! Taylor had begun developing self-control—an essential aspect of maturity as well as a fruit of the Spirit (Galatians 5:23). Self-control helps separate us from the animal kingdom, and it helps our children take responsibility for their actions. They don't have to act out feelings. They can express, reflect, symbolize, or delay gratification. Children can learn that they can't always control how they react emotionally, but they can control how they respond behaviorally.

What Kids Need to Understand
"It's Hard" Versus "I Can't"

Another aspect of learning to take responsibility for oneself is for the child to understand that *being unable* differs from *being uncomfortable.* Kids see the two as one. Therefore, what they don't enjoy, they think they can't do. So, since they can't do something they are uncomfortable doing, someone else needs to do it. And that someone else is the boundaryless parent.

Thinking that he can't do what he doesn't enjoy impedes a child's learning that his life and problems are his responsibility, not someone else's. He will either give up difficult things because they are too hard, charm someone else into doing them for him, or find shortcuts like cheating on exams.

It all starts with small things. Recently I found myself in one of these situations with Benny, our five-year-old. He had spilled his juice cup at dinner and, with help, was doing a good job of cleaning up the mess. When he was finally finished, he automatically held up the juicy paper towel for me to put into the trash can. Just as automatically, I reached out to take the paper towel. Then something stopped me. I think it was only because I have been writing this book.

I said, "Benny, what are we doing? You can get up from the table and throw the paper towel away." And Benny really had no problem with it. He didn't get angry or protest. He just got up and threw it away, and we resumed dinner. I think it was a new thought for both of us.

Benny and I had been in a dance in which he would hand off something to me, and I would take the ball and run with it for him. It hadn't occurred to me in that particular situation that he had two good legs and was a pretty good shot at hitting the trash can. He wasn't helpless and in need of adult rescue. And what was really significant about this for me is that it wasn't Benny's fault. It was mine.

Children will take every opportunity they can to shirk their responsibilities until we make taking ownership an expected lifestyle. As we will say in many ways throughout the book, you don't simply teach boundaries to your kids. Verbal instruction is never enough. You model boundaries. *You become boundaries with your kids.* In other words, your job is to become a person who structures his life around responsibility and reality. This is what develops your children's sense of responsibility.

Part of growing up is learning what we are responsible for and what we need the help of others on. Galatians 6 teaches a paradox: "Each one should carry his own load" (v. 5), but "carry each other's burdens" (v. 2). At first glance, it appears that we are to solve our problems and everyone else's! For some of us, this is how our life seems. But the Bible really doesn't teach that. The Greek words explain the difference. As we say in the book *Boundaries,* the "burdens" that we should bear for one another are the overwhelming "boulders" in life, such as financial, medical, or emotional crises. The "loads" that we need to carry ourselves are "knapsacks"—that is, the normal responsibilities of working, going to school, and fulfilling duties to our friends, family, and church.

Kids often see their knapsacks as boulders and want us to solve their problems for them. We need to frustrate this desire and build within them a sense that, while they are to ask for help in matters beyond them (transportation, opportunities to make money, crises), they are expected to handle many things on their own (grades, behavior, tasks).

This is the other end of responsibility. There certainly are things and problems with which children *do* need help. Life is difficult, and none of us can do alone all that is required of us. In fact, Lone Ranger types, who solve all their troubles in isolation, are emotionally ill, not healthy. The Bible teaches that we are to "strengthen the hands that are weak and the knees that are feeble" (Hebrews 12:12 NASB). All of us need the support, love, advice, and wisdom of others to navigate through life.

Your child needs to know it's okay to ask for help when she is in a crisis, is feeling overwhelmed, or has some problem she can't solve alone. You need to make your home an environment in which it's safe for her to come home and say, "I'm flunking math, and I can't understand the material," or "I got arrested," or "I'm pregnant." In these situations the family needs to surround the child and help her to solve her problems.

But even in these crisis situations, a child must still learn responsibility. She still has tasks. Here are her jobs:

- Being honest and humble enough to realize you have a problem instead of being proud or denying the problem
- Taking initiative to ask for help from others instead of withdrawing, or hoping it will go away
- Picking trustworthy people of character you can ask for help
- Doing your part to solve the problem
- Valuing and appreciating the help that's given
- Learning from the experiences so that you don't repeat them

This is the bad news in life: Even when we are unable to help ourselves, we still have a job to do. If you are hit by a car, you're a victim—but you still have to hobble to the physical therapist and do the exercises. If your best friend moves away, it's not your fault—but it's your job to find other people of character in whom to entrust your heart. There are very few "boulders" in life in which the child has no responsibility at all.

Loving Versus Rescuing

When I was in eighth grade, a new teacher substituted for our regular science teacher, Mrs. Southall, who was ill. The substitute was inexperienced and fragile, and Bill, one of the more popular boys, gave her a hard time. At one point, when her back was turned, he called the teacher a bad name, and she left the room crying.

When Mrs. Southall returned the next day, she was furious. She wanted to know who called the sub the foul name. No one would volunteer Bill's name, though we all knew. So Mrs. Southall went down the rows of desks and asked each of us individually by name if we knew. We couldn't avoid the issue; we had to lie or tell the truth. One by one, thirty kids all looked Mrs. Southall in the eyes and lied, including me.

Only one boy, a kid named Jay, said, "Bill did it." Bill was convicted and sentenced on Jay's testimony. And Bill was really angry at Jay for a long time. He and his friends ostracized Jay, so Jay suffered socially for what he did.

Years later, I asked Jay about his actions. Jay wasn't a teacher's pet or out to get points. He simply didn't agree that Bill should be rescued. "Bill was a friend of mine," said Jay. "But I just thought right was right and wrong was wrong. And I didn't think I would be doing him any favors by lying for him." I admire Jay's convictions. He risked his friend's rage and withdrawal to keep from rescuing him from his actions. Jay was differentiating between *help* and *rescue*.

Learning this distinction is one of the most important lessons in your child's course on responsibility. He is responsible *for* himself. He is responsible *to* others. He is to care about his family and friends and go out of his way to help them. But responsibility dictates that he refrain from protecting them from the consequences of their own actions.

Again, this does not come naturally to kids. They vacillate between enormous self-centeredness and incredible caretaking of friends. They don't know the difference between being responsible "for" themselves and "to" their friends. Especially in friendships, children often equate caring with protecting. (For example, a child may demand that his friend stand up for him even when he is wrong.)

Some of this confusion is part of the developmental process. That is, as kids begin to grow and separate from their home life, they are developing other social systems and structures to prepare them for leaving home. Especially during the later teen years, the center of their life is outside the home rather than inside it. This process involves bonding "with" friends and "against" parents. They feel that parents don't understand their feelings, problems, passions—and music. So they form tight cliques of soul mates and spend hours with them, sharing thoughts, feelings, and secrets.

This is a good thing for children. However, while you as a parent need to allow your kids to have their own lives and friends within reasonable limits, your kids still need to learn that the Law of Responsibility applies to their buddies as well as their families. Kids need to withstand the intense social pressure not to tell about a friend who is into drugs or cheats on exams. And in the same way, they need to learn how to say no to their friends' demands to solve their problems, take care of their feelings, and make them happy.

Children don't learn this from a book. Kids learn about loving and rescuing at home. When your child sees that Mom, Dad, and his siblings don't need him to parent them, he learns that he can love others without taking responsibility for them. He can enter freely into relationships knowing that he can obey the Law of Empathy but can also say no to those things that aren't good for him or are someone else's burden. Let him skin his knee and get up and get the Band-Aids without your rushing over to coddle him. Let him observe you having a bad day, but know that you'll take care of yourself.

As you help your child learn the difference between loving and rescuing, he will also be learning how to pick kids who don't need someone to take on their problems: kids of good character, kids to whom your child can say no without fear of losing the connection.

A major reason children rescue is that they have learned it's the only way to keep a friend. Help your child to pick better friends than that. I always pray a silent prayer of thanks when I watch my kids interacting outside the kitchen window in our backyard and see them disagree with their friends. Most of the friends they pick don't freak out when someone disagrees with them. Our children will need to make and keep friends like this for a lifetime.

It is easy to slip into allowing a child to rescue and become confused about responsibility. For example, a lonely parent will often make a child into a confidant, thinking, *Isn't it great that my daughter and I are best friends? I can tell her all my problems, and vice versa.* In reality, the child learns to parent the parent and risks approaching all relationships like this. We have seen hundreds of people in codependent marriages, "givers" who married "takers." In so many instances, the giver's childhood included one of the following:

- A lonely, needy parent
- An out-of-control parent who needed someone to help control him
- A parent who confused his child's needs with his own

Our kids aren't an annuity for our retirement, social system, or medical frailty. They are there for God and themselves. It's a good thing to be vulnerable with your child about your weaknesses and failures. This way they learn that adults aren't perfect. It's another thing to look to your child to meet your needs. Don't burden your children with your hurts. For example, don't look to your child to comfort your pain or be your best buddy; find adults for those needs. Your child has enough work to do in growing up. At the same time, learn the balance between helping him not to rescue but how to attend to the genuine needs of his family and friends. Learning to love begins with first receiving empathy, then understanding our duty to respect and care for others.

How can a child who is so small and weak have so much power over a grown-up? If you have ever seen a mom at the mercy of an out-of-control child in a supermarket, you have observed this dilemma. The next law of boundaries deals with this issue: helping your child own the real power he has and give up the power he shouldn't have.

— 6 —

I Can't Do It All, But I'm Not Helpless, Either
The Law of Power

When I (Dr. Townsend) was seven, I started reading *Tom Sawyer*, and I knew it was time to run away from home. Sick of my parents and siblings, I knew I could make it without them. So one Saturday, I found a stick and a red bandanna, into which I packed my basic survival tools: peanut butter sandwich, flashlight, compass, ball, and two small green plastic army action figures.

I left the house in the afternoon and walked a couple of blocks down the street to the woods. Resolutely, I trudged where no boy had ever gone before. The trail ended, and the brush got thick. I ate my sandwich. It got dark. I heard sounds. It was time to go home.

I remember walking back home thinking, *This is really crummy. I don't want to go home. Nobody's making me go home. But I need to go home.* There I was, wanting to be powerful and independent, yet faced with my own powerlessness.

Power and Children

At some time or another, most children have similar experiences. They think they are grown-up, strong, and without limitations. They become overconfident and cocky in their omnipotence. Then, if parents don't get in God's way, kids run into the reality that they don't have as much power as they thought. They have to make some adjustments to life, and they grow from the experience. They adapt to reality, which is the definition of mental health, rather than demanding that reality adapt to them, which is the definition of mental illness.

To develop appropriate boundaries, children need to have power, or the *ability to control something*. Power can range from putting a puzzle together to dancing in a recital, from solving a conflict to developing a successful friendship. Children's survival and growth in the world depends on an appropriate, reality-based appraisal of the following:

- What they do and don't have power over;
- The extent of their power over the things they do control; and
- How they adapt to the things they can't control.

For example, I was powerless over my need to get back home. I had to adapt to my lack of power by resigning myself to the fact that I was still a little boy. But I had power over how I felt. I disliked having to need my family. At least I had a little power there!

To observe the paradox of kids and power, consider an infant and her parents. Right out of the womb, an infant is completely helpless. In fact, a human infant is helpless longer than any baby animal is. At the same time, she wields enormous power over her parents. They rearrange their work schedules, home life, and sleeping routines around her. They carry her very gently. They are phobic about germs. They install a monitor in her bedroom to make sure she's breathing. For a period of time, she is the center of their life. Yet, if you were able to talk to the child, she wouldn't say, "I'm running this family around." Instead, she wavers between unpleasant states of terror, helplessness, and rage and pleasant states of safety, warmth, and love. She would probably say, "I have no power or control at all."

In this powerless state, a child has no power over herself, so God designed a system in which her parents give power to her and sacrifice for her until she can grow up enough to develop a sense of personal power.

Power, Powerlessness, and Boundaries

Learning the proper use of power helps children develop their boundaries. Mature people know what they have power over and what they don't. They invest themselves in the first and let go of the second. Your child needs to learn what he has power over, what he doesn't have power over, and how to tell the difference (to paraphrase the Serenity Prayer).

Children don't start off with a reality-based understanding of power. They think they can leap tall buildings in a single bound. They cheerfully run into the ocean, confident that they will tame the waves. And they fully expect that you and their friends will see life as they do.

Herein lies the first problem: A child is forever attempting to have power over things that aren't his. But *he can't set boundaries around that which isn't his property.* When he tries, the real owner will eventually tear down his fences. This is what happens when a child bullies his friends. If they are normal, they will protest or simply leave. So the child who thinks he is omnipotent becomes stuck in a perpetual loop, either making fruitless attempts to control what he cannot or finding weak people who will help him maintain his delusion. A classic adult case is the controlling husband and the compliant wife. He thinks he has power over her life. She participates in the illusion by going along to get along and not confronting him with his own impotence to own her. A child who never comes to terms with the limits of his power can become such a controlling husband.

The second problem the child faces is that *in trying to control the uncontrollable, he negates his ability to exercise power over what he does have.* He is so focused on the first that he neglects the second. In the example above, a child who is invested in "making" friends do what he wants will neglect taking control over himself, learning to accept their choices, adapting to them, grieving some desires, and so forth. God gives us power to do not what we want, but what is good and right.

In fact, learning to accept powerlessness has profound spiritual implications for your child. When we accept the reality of our human condition—that we are ultimately powerless to change our fallen state, yet totally responsible for being in it—we are driven to receive God's solution based on his Son's payment of a debt we can't pay. Children who grow up hanging on to their omnipotence and never coming to terms with their absolute failure may have difficulty seeing the need for a Savior. They are prone to think, *I just need to try a little harder.* Yet the Bible teaches that being powerless is a blessed state: "When we were still powerless, Christ died for the ungodly" (Romans 5:6).

What Is and Isn't the Child's

Parents have vivid memories of the power struggles they have had with their children. Kids assert their omnipotence in millions of arenas such as chores, clothing styles, privileges and restrictions, and friends. It's your job to help your children sort out what they do and don't have control of and the extent of their power. Keep in mind, also, that you most likely won't have willing pupils for the lessons. Just like adults, children don't like to be reminded of their limitations and may want to shoot the messenger. Keep a thick skin as you go about your divinely ordained duties.

Power over Myself

First, a child needs to understand what she can and can't do regarding herself. The table below lists a few of the important aspects of this:

I don't have the power to ...	I do have the power to ...
Survive without needing others	Choose whom I depend on
Do whatever I desire	Do what I am able
Avoid consequences	Adjust so as to minimize consequences
Avoid failure	Accept failure, learn, and improve

Denial of Dependency

Children don't like to be reminded that they need anyone but themselves. They want to make their own decisions, solve their own problems, and never have to ask you for help or support. They want independence so badly that they will often get into serious trouble before letting their parents know what's going on.

Two kinds of dependency often get confused here. *Functional dependency* relates to the child's resistance to doing the tasks and jobs in life that are his responsibility. This means he wants others to take care of things he should. For example, a teen asks his parents for spending money instead of getting a part-time job. Don't enable functional dependency. Allow the teen to feel the pinch of being broke. It will help him to apply for work.

Relational dependency is our need for connectedness to God and others. God has designed us to be relationally dependent; it is our life-maintaining fuel: "Pity the man who falls and has no one to help him up!" (Ecclesiastes 4:10). Relational dependency is what drives us to unburden our souls to each other and be vulnerable and needy. Then, when we are loved by God and others in this state of need, we are filled up inside. Because they need so much, children are especially relationally dependent. Over time, as they internalize important nurturing relationships, they need less; the love they have internalized from Mom and Dad and others sustains them. Yet, to our dying day we will always need regular and deep connection with emotionally healthy people who care about us.

You need to promote and encourage relational dependency in your child. Teach him that mature, healthy people need other people; they don't isolate themselves. Your child may also confuse the two types of dependency, thinking that if he asks for comfort and understanding, he is being a baby. Help him see that needing love isn't being immature. Rather, it gives us the energy we need to go out and slay our dragons.

You see that your child has a problem, but he may isolate himself in his omnipotent self-sufficiency. It's the old "How was your day?" "Okay" dialogue. Confront the isolation. Tell him you don't want to lecture him—you just want to know how he's feeling. Don't enable his illusion of not needing others.

One way you can help here is by waiting until you are invited to help. If you rush in and pick up a kid who falls down before she cries for you, she can easily develop a stance that *I am so powerful that I don't need Mom,* as she doesn't have to take responsibility for asking for help. Let her choose to ask. It's not easy to watch and wait while your child gets to the end of herself. It tears at any caring parent's heart. But it is the only way the child can realize her need for support and love, and her lack of total power to live without it.

While your child is learning how to need others, help him not to feel helpless in his relationships. Encourage him to express his wants, needs, and opinions to those with whom he is close. This is true especially in his relationship with you. He didn't choose to be in your family; that was your decision. He can have some choices in how to relate to you, however. For example, give him some leeway in establishing his own rhythm of when he needs to be close and when he needs distance from you. Don't be intrusive and affectionate when he clearly needs to be more separate. Yet don't abandon him when he needs more intimacy. Another example is to encourage him to share his feedback on family activities. He has input, and his input matters even though he doesn't have the final say-so.

Demanding Power over All Choices

Children think they have the power to do everything they set their mind to. No activity level is too much. They have an omnipotent illusion of their unlimited time and energy. A child doesn't recognize time constraints or "counting the cost" (Luke 14:28). For example, a kid might construct the following game plan for a Saturday:

9 a.m.: Soccer game	1 p.m.: Skating
10:30 a.m.: Movie	3 p.m.: Party
Noon: Hot dogs	5 p.m.: Another movie

Your child needs your help in this matter. Kids can easily expect too much of themselves, thinking they have power over their energy, time, and activity planning. They can develop boundary problems by overcommitting themselves and then having a shallow experience of too many things.

A friend of mine was this way as a child. Now, as a wife and mother, she still finds herself trying to stretch time like an accordion. She thinks she can take the kids to school, go shopping, have coffee with a friend, and clean the house before lunch. Instead, she finds herself rushed, frustrated, and chronically late. She is now trying to work through her illusion of total power over what she wants to do.

Within certain age and maturity parameters, help your child establish time and energy boundaries by setting up a system that breaks down if she does too much. For example, as an experiment, let her plan more than you would like. But factor in requirements such as

- A B+ average in school
- Four nights at home with family
- In bed, lights out by a certain time
- No signs of fatigue or stress

Give your child enough rope to hang herself, so that *she* chooses her destiny, not you. During my high school years I was so overcommitted with schoolwork, social activities, and sports I started showing signs of stress and fatigue. My parents sat me down one night and told me they thought I had mono. I was totally unaware that I was sick, and I was always grateful that they let me go as far as I did to experience my lack of omnipotence over my time and energy.

Avoiding Consequences

Part of your little angel's makeup is a criminal mind. He thinks he's powerful enough to avoid the results of his actions. He comes by it naturally: Adam and Eve thought they could hide from God! Kids will manipulate, lie, rationalize, and distort to avoid punishment.

Children need to learn to prevent bad consequences by taking control of their actions. When they think they can avoid getting caught, they no longer focus on self-restraint, they focus on getting away with it. The result is not character maturity, but character pathology.

Make honesty the norm in your home's daily culture, and set strong limits on dishonesty. Whatever the consequence for disobedience, set a worse one for deception. Whatever the reward for obedience, make a better one for honesty. Throw a party when your child fesses up to something. He needs to experience the reality that living in the darkness of deception will be much more painful than living in the light of exposure. This will help him move away from the illusion that he has the power to avoid reaping what he sows.

One family I know has a rule that if you tell on yourself, it's a certain penalty. But if someone else tells on you first, it's a worse punishment. While this has the built-in problem of developing fast-talking tattlers, it does correspond to America's present-day legal system, in which lawbreakers who turn themselves in are given more leniency than those who are caught.

Avoiding Failure

Born perfectionists, kids don't like to be reminded that they are products of the Fall. They often think they have the power to avoid making mistakes or failing. Your child needs to learn to grieve his lost perfection, accept his failures, learn from them, and grow. Growing up leaves no other option. You either deny your mistakes and repeat your life over and over again, or you admit them and work through them.

Disabuse your child of the notion she can get around failure. Make failure her friend. Talk about the dumb things you did at work or at home. Don't be defensive when a family member points out another mindless thing you did. Be careful not to give your child the impression that you love her perfect, performing parts more than you do her mediocre, stumbling parts. When you talk about her to your friends, include the quality of admitting failure among her other achievements. This information tends to get back to kids.

Power over Others

As you help your child give up his delusions of being able to perfectly control himself without failure, you will also need to help him with his similar delusions concerning his power over others. Remember the picture of the powerless/powerful infant? This is how children begin—and will stay unless you step in. The goal for your child is to give up the idea that he can control others and to concentrate on controlling himself. Remember that one of the fruits of the Spirit is self-control, not other-control (Galatians 5:23).

Babies need parents most of the time, and pretty much on demand. Otherwise they cannot survive. But as they grow older, they develop enough basic trust in others and enough confidence in their own abilities to solve their problems that they don't feel so desperate to have power over Mom and Dad. Still, children hold onto the idea that they can make others do what they want. They need love, encouragement to take responsibility, and limits on their omnipotence. You are the agent for these three ingredients.

When Ricky was in preschool, he had a dear best friend named David. They palled around all day together. At dinner one evening, Ricky told me sadly that David had a new best friend, Andy. David and Andy were now spending time together without Ricky. He was feeling left out and lonely. I worked on some problem solving with him.

"Why don't you talk to David about your feelings?" I suggested.

"I can do that."

"What do you think you should say to him?"

"I'll say, '*You have to like me.*'"

This is how kids think. Whether due to fear or a desire to be God, children think they have power over their family and friends. Here are some examples of how children try to have power over others and the responses you can make:

Attempt to Have Power over Others	Your Response
If I whine long enough, I'll get the toy.	Ask me once, and I'll decide. But whining gets an automatic no.
I can push my friends around.	They seem to avoid you now. Let's hold off on inviting people until you and I deal with this by coaching you on how to treat people.
If I am polite and helpful, I won't have to stay on restriction for my last curfew violation.	I'm glad your attitude is so good, but you are in for the duration of your sentence.
I can ignore your requests to clean up the family room.	I won't ask more than once, and you have fifteen minutes. After that, you miss the game with your friends.
I can intimidate you with my yelling and anger.	Your rage does bother me, and it's a big deal. So until you can be appropriate and talk to me respectfully, all privileges are suspended.
My hatred can destroy you.	You can make me uncomfortable and hurt my feelings. But your hatred doesn't injure me or make me go away.

In this way you help children give up their wish for power over you and others. As with any aspect of child rearing, the first time you give these responses, you probably won't be believed, and the situation will come up again. During the second or third attempt to resist your limits, disbelief may be followed by rage. Hang in there. After the children realize that your boundary is reality, you can discuss what's going on more calmly.

If the process is working, your child may begin feeling sad that he can't rule his relational world. Grief is good for him, as it allows him to let go of an unrealistic wish. However, help him see that, even though he can't have power over others, he isn't helpless, either. Your child needs to learn that he can *influence* others toward whatever he thinks is important. Control and influence are very different. Control denies the other's freedom; influence respects this freedom. Tell him, "If you disagree with some decision I am making, I welcome your opinion and suggestions as long as they are respectful. I will listen to them with an open mind, but only if you are willing to still accept my decision once I've thought about what you have said. You have to earn the right to be heard by your behavior."

The Injured Parent

If your child directs his rage or selfishness at you, it can be hurtful. Because you are closely connected to him, he has the power to make you feel bad. Don't, however, give in to the temptation to use that fact as a way to manipulate the child into taking care of your feelings. For example, some parents will say something like "If you yell, you make Mommy sad, and she needs you to help her be happy." This only increases the child's omnipotence and contributes to several other problems, such as

- Putting the child in the parent role
- Creating unnecessary guilt in the child
- Influencing the child to have contempt for the parent's fragility
- Making the issue one of the parent's feelings rather than the child's consequences

At the same time, the child needs to understand that he does hurt you and that you don't like that. This builds a sense of empathic responsibility in your kid. We all need to know that we can hurt people we value and that if we continue this in life, we will have problems making and keeping good relationships. This orients the child toward taking ownership of the power he has to affect others.

Principles of Power Development

The basic concepts to keep in mind as you work with your child on owning what is his and adapting to what is another's are summarized in the graph below:

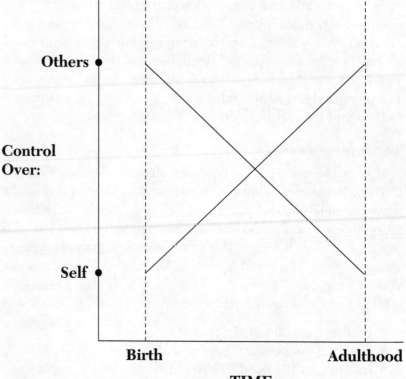

A child enters the world with almost no power over himself. To compensate, he exerts enormous energy in controlling his parents. Your job is to gradually increase his power over himself and decrease his attempts to control you and others.

Stay Connected, No Matter What

You are in the business of removing omnipotent power from your child to help her have real power over what is hers. In her mind, you are taking away something she needs. To help her tolerate the process, you will need to stay emotionally present with her. Empathize with her fears of being helpless, her frustration that she can't control her friends' reactions, and her concerns about failure. Empathy is especially important when you are dealing with her attempts to control you. Tell her, "I may get angry or hurt while we go through this, but I won't go away. No matter what, I am here for you, even if I disagree with you and have to set limits with you. Now let's get to work on this."

Don't Be an Omnipotent Parent

Help your child accept the limits of his power by accepting yours. Admit your failure, weakness, and limitations. But, in addition, own what power you do have. In doing this, give your child as much freedom as possible and control him as little as possible. "I'll make you stop" is sometimes necessary for very young children or for emergencies. However, it's much better to say, "I can't make you stop, but I can tell you what will happen if you don't." Then don't make empty threats. Follow up on promised consequences. That's where your true power resides. You can't make a child behave, but you can structure choices and consequences that help the child choose rightly.

Be a Parent Who Makes Free Decisions

Be "uncontrollable"—that is, be a parent whose choices aren't dictated by your child's responses. His feelings and desires matter to you because you love him. But you are the boss, and you're making the choices you deem best because you are accountable to a higher Boss (2 Corinthians 5:10).

I've seen parents vacillate on their decisions when their kids freak out. They don't base their actions on values, but on conflict

management. This leads children to conclude that they have a
great deal of power over their parents. And they are right.

If you aren't sure about your child's request, simply say no.
If you can't say yes wholeheartedly, you may be giving grudgingly
or under compulsion (see 2 Corinthians 9:7). Moreover, remember that the parent who says no and then changes her mind is a
hero, but the one who says yes and then no is a traitor.

Being a free parent also means not reacting to your child's
ploys to have power over you. If you need your child to behave
a certain way, you have just given her power over you. For example, kids know certain tones of voice to use and names to call
parents that will either send them over the edge or make parents feel warm and generous. Many are the dads whose resolve
not to spoil a daughter melts when she begins doing her little-
girl and wonderful-daddy routine. The key is not to need anything from your child, such as appreciation, support, respect,
or understanding. You should require certain standards of behavior, not because you need that, but because your child does. Get
your needs met from other people in your life, and free your
child to be totally herself with you. Then you can work together
to smooth her rough edges.

Work Toward Giving Your Child Self-Governing Power

Keep in mind that parenting is a temporary job. You have
been invested with trustee power while your child is growing
up in your care. But gradually, as he becomes more able to take
on responsibility, you should be handing the reins of his life over
to him. The statement "I'll always be your parent" is true in one
sense, but not in another. You will always have that heritage,
but you won't always have that responsibility. Your goal is a
mutual affection between two adults, not a permanent one-up
position.

The trick here is to know what you can let the child handle
that takes him out of his comfort zone but is not beyond his
maturity. Stretch him, but don't break him. I remember calling my parents at the beginning of my freshman year in college.

"What courses should I take?" I asked anxiously.

"What was your high school grade point average?" my father asked.

"It was good enough."

"Well, if you're smart enough to be in a university, I'll bet you're smart enough to figure out what courses to take."

It took me a semester of underwater basket-weaving courses and some bad grades to learn how to choose course work that made sense for me. But I did learn, and I began enjoying college because I had taken responsibility for my decisions. Thanks, Dad, for the frustration!

Limit Omnipotence, But Encourage Autonomy

Children need to know they can't do everything they want. However, this doesn't mean they must be slaves to you or anyone else. They need to develop a sense of autonomy, or free choice over their decisions. Don't fall into the mistake of removing all power from your children. They need all the authentic power they can get. A three-year-old, for example, can choose a certain toy at a toy store within certain financial and safety parameters. A teen should have the power to choose friends, clothes, and music, also within certain parameters. You are the laboratory in which your children learn the difference between omnipotence and autonomy. They will bounce both extremes around with you, and your job is to help them develop healthy self-control.

As much as possible, include your child in decisions about him. Talk to him about school, church, finances, and problems in ways that don't violate the child-parent boundary (don't make him a peer or confidant for your problems). Ask for his input, especially with respect to your boundaries and consequences concerning him. Listen to him, and if he makes sense, use the information to adapt some stance you've taken. This doesn't undermine your authority, and it helps him to feel less like a child.

Sometimes having kids set their own consequences can be a good learning experience. Quite often, children are stricter on themselves than you would be! However, always maintain the final authority in case you have a kid who's more into grace than responsibility!

Conclusion

Power can either heal or harm your child. She needs the power that comes from a realistic sense of self-control, and she needs to give up the desire to have absolute power over herself and her relationships. A reality-based understanding of the true power will provide her with a foundation for respecting, setting, and keeping boundaries. Help her develop her treasures with the "spirit of power, of love and of self-discipline" (2 Timothy 1:7).

But what does a parent do when her child uses his power to intrude on the boundaries of others? We'll deal with this in the next chapter as we address the Law of Respect.

— 7 —

I'm Not the Only One Who Matters

The Law of Respect

Remember when you left your toddler with a baby-sitter? How many times did you get this response from her: "Well, Mom and Dad, I can see that you really need some time for yourselves away from me. I've been hoping you'd do that. You really should think of yourselves more often. Well, have a great time and don't worry about me at all. I need to learn to take care of myself and respect others' privacy and needs"?

Or have you ever heard this response from your eight-year-old: "Oh, Mom, I understand. Even though I really want ice cream now and want you to stop at 31 Flavors, I can see that getting home is really important to you. Let's do it your way"?

Or the teen version: "I can understand why I can't go on the ski trip. Giving me money for that trip would put a strain on the family budget. I'll go do some odd jobs around the neighborhood and earn it myself."

Sound familiar? We doubt it. The common denominator in all these situations is respect for others' existence, needs, choices, and feelings. This respect for others does not come naturally. It is learned. Have you ever been in a relationship with an adult who cannot respect your boundaries? It is a tiring and difficult thing. And learning this truth is very important for your children. If they grow up not respecting the boundaries of others, their future will be fraught with pain.

Every child comes into the world wanting things his way, and he has little regard for what others need. Not only does he want *things* his way, he wants *people* his way. He wants not only to

103

make all the rules for himself, but also to dictate the lives, possessions, feelings, and freedoms of others. In short, he comes into the world thinking that others exist only for him, possessing no life of their own. Your task—and the subject of this chapter—is to cure him of his natural disrespect for the boundaries of other people.

Respecting Others' Boundaries

To respect the boundaries of others and to get along with others, children must learn several things:

1. To not be hurtful to others
2. To respect the no of others without punishing them
3. To respect limits in general
4. To relish others' separateness
5. To feel sad instead of mad when others' boundaries prevent them from getting what they want

A child does not come into the world doing any of the above, so your work is cut out for you.

Good Lessons: Don't Hurt Others, Don't Trespass, and Don't Punish Their "No"

As we said in chapter 3, the best way of teaching a child to respect others is for you to have good personal boundaries of your own. This means you are not going to allow yourself to be treated with disregard. Your boundaries as a parent are the ones that your child will internalize. If you say no when your children do not respect your own personal boundaries or limits, they learn to respect others and their limits. If you don't, they don't.

Here's an example of eleven-year-old Billy's disrespect of his mom's limits:

"Mom, I'm going down to Joey's to play hockey. See ya later."

"No, Billy. You can't go. It's time to do your homework."

"Come on, Mom! Everyone's going. I can do my homework later."

"Billy, I understand you want to go, but we agreed that if you went swimming, you would work on homework before dinner."

"Yeah, but I could do it after dinner."

"An agreement is an agreement. I don't want to talk about it anymore."

"You're just stupid. You don't understand anything. You're a big, fat, stupid."

If this sounds familiar, don't fret. Normal children naturally hate limits when you first set them. Your test is what are you going to do when the child expresses disrespect and hatred. It is normal for disrespect to occur, but it is not normal for it to continue. The cure is empathy and correction, then consequences.

Empathy and Correction

- "Billy, I understand that you're really disappointed, but that's not the way to talk to me. Calling me 'stupid' is not okay. It hurts my feelings. It is okay to be sad or mad, but I won't allow name calling."
- "Billy, I understand that you're upset. But when you call me stupid, how do you think that makes me feel?" (Wait for an answer so he has to think about how another person feels.) "How do you feel when people call you names? Would you like to be treated that way?"
- "Billy, I hear that you're ticked, and when you talk to me more respectfully, I'll be glad to listen. I won't listen to people who call me stupid. If you are upset about something, tell me in a different way."
- "Billy, please think about what you just said and say it better."

When correction is followed by an apology, sufficient self-correction, and repentance, the child learns respect. If the child does not apologize, repent, and correct himself or if this is a pattern, consequences should follow.

Consequences

- "Billy, I asked you to not speak to me that way. I don't listen to talk like that because it hurts my feelings. So you can go to your room and think about a better way to say it."

- "Billy, until you can stop the sarcasm, you can go somewhere else where someone wants to listen to it. I don't. Go away."
- "Billy, if you are bugging all of us this badly with your attitude, I have no idea what you are doing out in the neighborhood. You better stay in for a while to think about how to talk more nicely to people."

Notice that, as much as possible, we connect the consequence to the trespass. In this instance, the trespass is relational. Billy is acting in a way people do not like. So the eventual consequence is losing access to people because of his behavior.

Notice also that Billy can't turn anything into a control issue. Mom is just stating her limits and what the consequences are. She is not shaming Billy or putting him down. She is stating what he really did. His choices are preserved. He can be a jerk if he wants to, but his mother has clearly stated what it is going to cost him. She is preserving his freedom and his choices and is being loving in the process. Those three ingredients—freedom, choice, and responsibility—are all being preserved in the relationship.

Billy finds out what is important about poor interpersonal behavior:

1. It hurts people.
2. It will cost you in your relationships.

As much as possible, make sure you stay in control of yourself, as this is what boundaries are all about. Three things need to happen here. First, you will not subject yourself to abuse. So when Billy talks to you that way, you, as a person with good boundaries, put limits on your listening, and then he has no one to talk to if he is going to act that way. (This is also effective with younger children who have temper tantrums. Tell them that they can be angry if they want to, but they must be angry in their own room. You don't want to hear the noise.)

Second, your child learns that his behavior hurts other people. Most children do not like the idea of hurting someone. They fight rules and limits, but they understand pain. Express to them that what they said was mean and that it makes you sad. You are beginning to teach them the Golden Rule, which is a morality based on empathy—that is, based on their awareness and concern for how the other person feels: "Love your neighbor as yourself" (Matthew 22:39). To treat others as we would want to be treated involves understanding how our behavior feels to other people. Children can soon understand that they would not want to be treated a certain way. Do not do this with guilt messages, but with an exploring tone as you say, "How do you feel when someone at school talks to you like that?" Have them think and answer, and then say, "Well, that is how I feel as well when you do it to me. I don't like it either."

Third, if the behavior is not self-correcting—which in the beginning it may not be—it has to cost the children something. A relational cost can be helpful. In other words, since they have hurt or have been disrespectful to a person, the cost is a loss of time with this person. Send the children away, and do not interact with them while they are acting that way. Tell them you think they need some time to think of a better way to talk to you, and then you will be willing to listen. "Acting mean" equals "acting mean alone." "Acting nicely" equals "having someone to listen." Listen to anger, but not to meanness.

What About Others?

The same principles apply with people other than you. In general, when possible, don't get involved in children's disputes with one another or with other adults. They need to learn how to work out these disagreements on their own. This also avoids the triangulation of a child's playing one parent against the other, or playing the parent against others outside the home.

Mary's thirteen-year-old son, Stephen, had an attitude problem. Once, he and a few friends were playing in the backyard when she heard the boys arguing. She fought her impulse to correct Stephen when she heard his "attitude" rearing its head again, although it broke her heart to hear it. The old Mary would have stepped in and tried to play peacemaker and help Stephen in his disputes with friends or siblings. But this time she decided to let him work it out on his own.

Soon Stephen came into the house alone. He was quiet, and he went in to turn on the television. When Mary tried to strike up a conversation, he did not seem very talkative. She surmised that things had not gone well with his friends.

"Where did your friends go?" she asked.

"Oh, they had to go," Stephen mumbled.

"It's pretty early. Why did they have to go?"

"They just did, that's all!" Stephen said, trying to avoid further conversation.

"Are you sure?"

Stephen looked sad. Mary knew this was a difficult moment for both of them. In the old days, when her toolbox consisted of just compassion but no boundaries, she would have tried to cheer him up and make him feel better. But after learning the formula of empathy and reality, she took a deep breath and tried to apply both.

"Stephen, did something happen to make Justin and Robbie want to go home?"

Soon Stephen came out with the story of having to have things his way. In reality, however, he wasn't owning up to his responsibility in the dispute and instead was inviting Mom to join him in blaming it on his friends: "It's not my fault! They didn't want to do the fun stuff. We had already played that game."

But this time Mary let reality be reality and just empathized with his pain.

"Stephen," she said lovingly, "you're feeling crummy because you are all alone. That's what happens when you always want things your way. You can always have things your way, but your friends won't want to be around you. If you share and compromise, you'll have friends to be with. It's tough to be alone. I understand. I feel for you. So, maybe it is good to think about whether having your own way all the time is that important to you or not. You can always do what you want to do, but you are going to be very lonely if you choose that path."

Using empathy and allowing him to feel the pain of loneliness, Mary let the reality of limits teach Stephen a lesson on respecting other people's boundaries. Within a year, after suffering more incidents like this one, Stephen changed. He was sharing with others at last.

Letting the reality of the child's world teach him and having the empathy and limits of the parent to support the learning process make up the best recipe for learning to respect boundaries. Doing this is difficult for parents, however. Most want to lecture or shame the child, or rescue him by blaming the school or other children. The wise parent lets the child's world teach him the lessons of life and then empathizes with his pain. Then he learns to respect the outside world's limits as well as his parents'. Asking Susie how she is going to work out her problem with her teacher is a much better approach than storming the school and working it out for her or, in most cases, punishing her at home for a problem she has at school.

Be aware that there are times when—just as in some adult disputes—the law has to be called in. The biblical principle is that God's children try to work out their differences before going to court (Luke 12:58). Sometimes, if we adults cannot work out our problems, we go to the law, and the courts help us come to a settlement. That settlement may involve consequences. For children, the "law" that is called in is a parent. Parents sometimes have to intervene and resolve the dispute, but only when all attempts by the child have not worked. Children must learn that they have to respect other people's property, or it is going to cost them. There can be consequences. But remember, if you work out all of their disputes, they will not learn the problem-solving skills they will need when you are gone.

Respecting Limits in General

A limit is generally not loved the first time around—or for that matter, the first several times around. As the Bible says, "No discipline seems pleasant at the time, but painful" (Hebrews 12:11). We protest limits as human beings. They limit our wish to be God. When you say no to children, they not only lose out on something they want, but they also find out that they are not in control of the universe. This discovery bugs them more than not getting to watch TV. Don't forget that it's normal for children to protest limits.

The problem arises when you get caught up in the protest. You feel as if you either have to defend the limit or punish the protest. Neither option is very helpful. Remember, *the limit is reality if you keep it.* It *is* the boundary. So children will respect the limit because it is real and it is not going away. After children protest, reality is still reality, and their protest will give in to sadness and adjustment if you do not get in the way. For this to happen, children need to have two ingredients present: the limit and love. If they have both, they can internalize the reality of limits in a nonadversarial way, and the limits become internal limits, structure, and self-control.

But if you argue with or condemn the child, then reality is no longer the problem. You are. Plus, no loving parent is there to help your child deal with reality, so she is in double trouble if you get into an argument or become condemning. She rejects the reality internally, and she hates you, since you are now the adversary.

Let's see what the two approaches look like. The first is the parent who gets caught up in the protest. The second is the one who responds with both love and limits.

Scenario One

"No, Kathy, you can't go to the movies today."

"That's not fair! Marcia's going. I hate your stupid rules."

"Kathy, that's a bad attitude. After all the things I have let you do, the least you could do is stop arguing with me."

"It isn't fair! All the other kids get to go. Michael gets to go more than me."

"I let you go to lots of things this week. Don't give me all that stuff about I don't let you do anything. Don't you remember when you went the other day?"

"But I want to go today. You don't even care!"

"I do care. How could you say that? All I ever do is cart you around from one place to the other. How can you say I don't care? Now straighten up your attitude, or you aren't going anywhere for a week!"

Scenario Two

"No, Kathy, you can't go to the movies today. You have to do your chores first."

"That's not fair! Marcia's going. I hate your stupid rules."

"I know. It's frustrating when you don't get to go to the movies again."

"But I want to go today. You don't even care!"

"I know you're frustrated and angry. It's tough to have to work before you have fun. I feel that way, too."

"I hate living here! I don't ever get to do anything."

"I know. It's hard to miss the movies when you really want to go."

"Well, if you know so much, then let me go."

"I know you want to. It's tough. But, no."

"But if I miss this one, there won't be another sneak preview this summer."

"That's sad. It's a long time till next summer. I can see why you hate missing it so much."

Finally the child gets bored with not getting anywhere, either with moving the limit or frustrating the parent, and she gives up. She must accept reality.

Notice that in this second scenario, Mom is not explaining or defending or shaming for the "pain of the moment." She is keeping the limit and empathizing with how Kathy is feeling. There is nothing for Kathy to argue about, nor is there any harshness or punishment from Mom. Just love and limits. Empathy is the rock on which Mom needs to stand when setting a limit. Kathy is not interested in explanations, anyway. They would not help, because she is really frustrated and angry. If Mom realizes that she owes Kathy love and empathy *only*, and Mom keeps the limit, then the limit becomes reality. If she does not let her own anger, shame, or justification get in the way, the limit becomes the real adversary, not Mom. Her empathy keeps her out of a power struggle with Kathy.

Parents get into trouble when they don't empathize with their child's pain. They either overidentify with the pain of the child and give in, or they get angry at the child's pain and go to war. Empathy and keeping the limit is the answer for both extremes. You may even want to arm yourself with these empathic statements.

- I understand how frustrating this must be for you.
- I bet that's a bummer, since other kids are getting to go.
- I know. I hate it, too, when I have to work instead of doing things I want to do.
- That's really sad, to miss something you were really counting on.
- I know, I know. It's hard.
- I know. I would rather be playing tennis than doing the wash. Isn't this the worst?

Pretty soon the child gets the picture that his protest is not going to move your limit or get a reaction out of you. These are the child's goals at the moment, because he wants two things:

1. He wants reality to change, and
2. He wants his parent to feel the pain he's feeling.

So, your job is to neither change the limit nor get frustrated. Stay firm and stay empathic; do not become angry or punitive. Protest will give way to reality, and the child will begin to feel the most important thing he can learn to feel about the limits of reality: sadness.

Sadness and Loss in the Face of Reality

Sadness is the sign that protest has given way to reality and that the child has begun to give up the battle. All of us must learn to do this with limits we encounter: Accept the loss of what we want and cannot have, and move on. The person who learns to move past protest to acceptance has learned an important character lesson: "Life is sad sometimes. You don't always get what you want. Too bad for me. Now I must go on."

When you think of adults you know who are stuck protesting a situation in life that they cannot change, you can begin to see how miserable are the people who have never learned this lesson. They cannot let things go, probably because they did not learn as children how to lose things and be sad. Empathy along with reality leads to acceptance and the ability to move on.

With some children you may need to sit down and talk to them at another time when the arguments are not happening. "I notice that sometimes when I say no to you, it is really tough for you. Do you want to talk about it? Do you think that I don't understand or let you do enough? If there is something between us, I want us to talk it out. Have I hurt you in some way?" In the heat of the protest is not the time to do this. Just give the limit and empathy.

Respecting Separateness

Our freedom and separateness from one another is one of the most important aspects of relationship. We need to be able to respect separateness from the people we love. This lesson begins in toddlerhood with the increasing separateness of Mom and Dad from the child, and vice versa. A child will cry and protest at being left and not responded to immediately. Parents who give in inappropriately to this perceived abandonment and let the child control them are teaching many bad lessons.

If children have had the proper nurture and are getting enough connection and love, they need to learn to tolerate separation. When they scream and cry, they need to be empathized with and left. They will learn to accept their individuality and relish it as they are forced to deal with it. This does not mean leaving a child with a true need, especially in infancy. True needs must always be answered.

When needs are met, children have to learn also that at times they are going to be separate from their loved one, and that this is a normal part of life. If empathized with and made to deal with this reality, they will learn that separateness is okay.

They Need Separateness, Too

Allow children their own separateness. To teach them to respect yours, you have to respect theirs. Give them age-appropriate freedom, and do not require them to be at your side at all times. Whether it is the freedom of a toddler to explore a safe area, a school-age child to go into the neighborhood, or a teen to date, their own space to live and make choices is important. As they get older, they will want and need more space, and as long as they handle it appropriately, they should have it. Do not overstep their privacy and space when you don't need to.

Their Space

A child's room is a good example of this separateness. We recommend teaching and requiring young children to clean up and keep their room reasonably neat. But the older they get, the more freedom they will want to manage their own space. Give it to them, but do not enable their irresponsibility if they blow it. If they have trouble finding things, for example, don't rescue them. Also, don't allow them to be slobs in common areas, for respecting those areas of the house provides the basis for learning to be a good neighbor. They can have their own space and live how they want to within limits. (Even the fire department will come issue you a citation if you don't observe hazardous limits as an adult. So, even though their room is their own space, they can lose sovereignty over it if they step over certain lines of safety.)

Their Time

Time is another example of separateness. As long as they are not endangering themselves, children should be able to control their own time and choices within age-appropriate limits. Younger children, under school age, need a lot of structure with their time, but within that structure they can use it as they choose. They are mostly learning that playtime ends, for example, and bedtime begins. School-age children learn that they can play after homework is done. Teens have to manage their own time, but the limits force them to manage it better. As soon as they are old enough to know how, put children in charge of being on time for things like school, church, and dinner, and completing things on time like chores and homework. If they mis-manage time, let them pay the consequences.

If you spend years nagging your children about getting ready for things, they will never learn time boundaries. Time limits are only real if you let them be real for the child. Do not nag! Do not remind too often! You are not a clock! Make sure they know how to tell time, tell them what time things happen, and let them get ready on time. If they don't, they have a problem. They may miss a few dinners, outings, or days at school, but they soon will learn what time really means.

If they have a pattern of not coming to dinner on time, they will get no food after dinner is done. Clarify your boundaries: "I will be serving dinner from 7:00 to 7:30 P.M. After that, the kitchen closes to those who have not eaten." Let them solve their own problems of going to bed hungry, missing the bus, or not being ready on time for something they wanted to go to. It won't take many instances of missing things for them to learn. But if you nag and try to control their separateness by not letting them manage the freedom themselves, they will never learn that time limits are real.

Their Choice of Friends

If your children are hanging out with kids you would not choose, just talk to them about their choice of friends (unless they are in danger, as explained below). Here are some suggestions:

- How does Sammy make you feel?
- Do you like to be treated like that? I wouldn't want to be around someone who doesn't respect my opinions.
- What is it you like about him? I usually don't like to be around people who always want their own way.
- I hope you are able to influence him for the better.
- I have friends who have different values, too. Do you find it difficult to not be influenced by them? What do you do when they want you to do something you don't believe in?

Sometimes your children's choice of friends may be danger-ous, and you have to act. But such choices mean that something more is going on. If a child is choosing hurtful people for friends, look for patterns of depression and discouragement or problems with passivity. If you see a pattern, seek professional help.

Their Money

Children need to have money they can spend for their own things, and then when the money is gone, it's gone. No more. Children need to learn what adult life will require them to know: Money is limited. The best way for them to learn this is to experience the limits of money firsthand. However, one of two things usually happens: Either children aren't given control over their own money and required to live within its limits, or parents give them so many handouts that they don't have to live within monetary limits. Parents often have difficulty watching a child go without something because she has already spent all her money.

But like the rest of teaching to respect reality, empathize; don't lecture. "I know. I feel crummy when I spend all of my money before the month runs out too. I have to go without things I need. I hate it when I do that."

Their Clothing and Appearance

Clothes and hairstyles should be a child's choice, unless these choices put the child in danger. For example, certain apparel can mean being in a gang or can imply promiscuity. Then you must step in. But until then, let children choose their own clothing and hairstyles. The sooner they learn to manage themselves and their separateness, the better. Generally, real-world consequences will coach them. If their clothes are too weird, the school yard will tell them. If their social circle does not ostracize them for the way they wear their hair, let them wear it as they wish. Your parents didn't like it when you dressed or wore your hair like Elvis, the Beatles, or Led Zeppelin either!

Concentrate on more important things like values, skills, love, honesty, and treatment of other people. Let your children manage their own separateness in appearance. A friend of mine once said, "When I figured out that his wearing an earring was his form of being different from me, I let him wear it. I did not want him to have to choose something destructive to prove he was his own person." Usually clothing and appearance say two things: "I belong to some group," and "I am different from my parents and can make my own choices." As long as this fits with the requirements of the places they have to go, let them have their way. (This does not mean that you have to like it! You have your own tastes. too. Just don't give them grief over theirs. It's their hair, after all.)

Your Separateness from Them

In addition to your children's separateness from you, you have to be separate from them. Parents who do not have a life apart from their kids teach the kids that the universe revolves around them. Do not be afraid of having your own nights out, your own trips without them as they get older, your own times alone, and your own space. From early on, it is important for a child to learn that Mom wants to read, not play right now. I have a friend who says to her young son at times like that, "I am reading and having fun. You are responsible for your own fun. Now go and make some." Or, "I know you're not through talking, but I'm through listening. I want to do my puzzle. Go play."

Parents who do not say no to their child's wish to be continually by their side are teaching him that he cannot exist on his own and that the world revolves around him. Later, this same child will not be comfortable allowing the one he loves to have her own sense of separateness, and he will try to control her. Meet the child's needs, then require him to meet his own while you meet yours. Empathize with the frustration, but keep the separateness.

How Are You Doing?

Children tend to be mirrors in which you can see yourself. They reflect your behavior, habits, attitudes, and ways of seeing and negotiating life. So before you do all the things in this chapter to teach your child to respect boundaries, make sure you are respecting theirs and others. Remember the goals of the Law of Respect:

- Don't hurt others.
- Respect the no of others without punishing them.
- Respect limits in general.
- Relish others' separateness.
- Feel sad instead of mad when you do not always get what you want.

Here are some helpful questions to ask yourself about how well you obey the Law of Respect:

1. When you hurt your children, do you own the behavior and apologize? Do you tell them you were just thinking of yourself and you're sorry? Do you ask for their forgiveness?

2. When your spouse or children say no to something you want, do you punish them by anger, manipulation, or withdrawal of love? May your children say no to you in matters they should have freedom in? Do you give them choices about managing their own lives? If you want them to play baseball, and they like soccer, are they free to say no to you? What if they do not agree with you on all your thoughts about God? Are they free to have separate opinions about their faith?

3. How do you deal with limits in general? Do you always try to "get around" the rules, and are you modeling that for your children? Do you accept appropriate limits or are you teaching your children that rules are good for everyone except you?

4. Do you relish the separateness of others? Are they allowed to have a life apart from you? Are you allowing your children to grow in independence and separateness from you? Do you love their freedom, or hate it?

5. When you don't get what you want from your children or others, do you get mad, or sad? Do you protest their choices with anger, or accept them with sadness? When things do not go your way, do you throw a temper tantrum, or do you feel sad and move on?

The ones who are shown respect are the ones who have the greatest chance of learning respect. You can't ask from your children what you aren't willing to give to them. Modeling respect for others and for the limits of reality will go further than any techniques you will ever learn.

The Result

The Law of Respect teaches children that the world does not belong to only them and they have to share it with others. They are learning to be good neighbors and to treat their neighbors as they would want to be treated. They don't always get things their way, and they are okay when they don't. They can tolerate not being able to move a limit. They can hear no from others without a fight. And they can tolerate that others have lives separate from them.

Remember, the path looks like this:

- Children protest the limit.
- They try to change the limit and punish the one setting it.
- You hold on to the limit, applying reality and empathy.
- Children accept the limit and develop a more loving attitude toward it.

This will not happen in a day. It is a process that will go through difficult seasons. But if you hang in there with love and limits until the very end, your loving discipline will produce a "harvest of righteousness and peace for those who have been trained by it" (Hebrews 12:11). And for their future and the future of the ones who will love them, your children will be living according to the Golden Rule of treating others in the way they would want to be treated. Life will be a lot better for them *and* for the ones they love.

But we all know that there are good and bad reasons for showing respect for others. Some people treat others well out of selfishness, guilt, or fear, for example. We want your children to learn loving and responsible behavior out of more positive motivations than these. The next chapter will teach you how to accomplish that.

— 8 —

Life Beyond "Because I'm the Mommy"

The Law of Motivation

On a father-son outing recently, I (Dr. Townsend) overheard a conversation between two dads that became a learning experience for me.

"I'm really having problems with Randy's attitude lately," said the first dad. "He'll take out the trash or do his homework after I tell him to, but he gripes and grumbles a lot about it. His motives aren't right."

There was a silence. Then the second dad replied: "Ed, sorry, but you need someone else's shoulder to cry on. My Mack has yet to find the trash can."

Two different dads, two different issues. One kid had crummy motives and attitudes. The other wasn't up to this problem yet.

At first blush, you may be wondering what motivation has to do with helping your child develop boundaries. This is especially true if you are in the second dad's situation. Many of you are struggling with out-of-control, defiant, passively withdrawn, or argumentative and manipulative kids. You're not looking for good motives. You're trying to find a way to get your children to mind you and become more responsible. Motive seems a long way away. "Let me get this kid under control," you plead, "then I'll worry about helping him with his motivation."

Motives drive our behaviors. They are the internal "because" behind the external actions we perform. As the Bible teaches, out of our hearts proceed all sorts of wicked deeds (Mark 7:20–23). If the behavior is the problem, it gets the attention. If you have a fire in your living room, you're more concerned about putting it out than where it came from.

But wait! Two very important issues revolve around the question of motives. First, once you have your child's attention, motives will become crucial. A child will clean her room because she won't get a movie that weekend unless she does. But when that same child turns twenty, she will need other reasons for keeping her place neat.

Motives, as we will see, develop in stages in a child's character. Immature motives, such as fear of pain and consequences, help young children. But parenting involves more than helping a child develop ownership over her behavior. You want your child to do the right things for the right reasons, not simply to avoid punishment. She needs to learn to be a loving person (see 1 Timothy 1:5).

Suppose you want your son to do his homework. He gets up from the table several times, dawdles, and finds ways to avoid it. You stand over him, nagging him until he finishes.

You may win the skirmish, but you have lost the war. Your son's motive for finishing his homework is to get you off his back, not so he will get a decent grade. What do you suppose will happen tomorrow night if you leave his side?

So many parents are stuck in this dilemma. They can rant, rave, and threaten, and the kids will stay in line *as long as the parents are standing over them.* But don't go off on a weekend trip when they're teens—they won't be trustworthy. Thousands of stories are told of good Christian parents being devastated by the news that their college kids have engaged in many activities never permitted at home. Some friends of mine were heartbroken to find that their freshman daughter had gotten pregnant at the Christian college they had sent her to. The girl was behaving like a very young child who has just been given enormous freedom. As they dealt with the issue, my friends realized that they had wanted the college to keep the same guard on her they had—an impossible task. The external restraint on her impulses (her parents) never became part of her character. Behavior dictated from the outside marks a child, not a young adult. The Bible teaches that in our spiritual journey we need a tutor called the law until we have entered a faith relationship with God and are motivated by higher principles (Galatians 3:24–25).

The second issue revolving around motives has to do with parenting tactics. A tired, desperate mom or dad will often resort to crazy strategies to get an unruly child to change. They may send guilt messages or threaten a loss of love. And while they may bring a temporary détente in the Cold War, these tactics never pay off in the long run. Appeals to improper motives not only do not work, but also hurt your child.

Do you remember how you felt when your mom or dad withdrew in silence when you disagreed or disobeyed? Many of today's parents have spent a lifetime suffering from the fruits of this manipulation. They have married and been controlled by guilt-producing spouses. They feel powerless with and resentful of shaming bosses and friends. Parents who love their child want to spare him the inner turmoil of forever trying to keep another person stable and happy.

So motivations are important in helping your child learn about boundaries. How does a parent help a child develop the right motive for love and good works?

The Goal: Love and Reality

My wife and I recently traveled to Sweden, where I spoke at a conference on spiritual issues. For a week we were guests in the home of the pastor and his wife who were hosting the conference. During that time we got to know not only them, but also their three daughters, ages eight to sixteen.

We were also impressed by how their home operated. After each meal, each girl knew her job. Without a word from her parents, each would get up, clear the table, wash the dishes, or clean the kitchen. So quiet and efficient were they that I looked around in surprise at a clean room, unaware of how it got that way. Now, these kids weren't robots by any means. They were vocal and opinionated, and they had their own personalities. But the home ran like a machine.

I asked one of the girls, "Why do you do your chores without complaining?" After a pause, she said, "Well, I like to help; and I also want my sisters to do their jobs!"

Well, before you go into a funk about how hard it is to get your kids to do chores, look at my Swedish friend's answer. She was talking about motivation. First, she was driven by love for her family: She liked to help. Second, she was influenced by the demands of reality: If she did her job, most likely her sisters would, too, and she wouldn't have to do extra work. This is a perfect picture of what you want to develop in the soul of your child: a desire to do the right things and to avoid the wrong ones because of empathic concern for others and because of a healthy respect for the demands of God's reality. These are the hallmarks of a child who will grow up into an adult who freely chooses her responsibilities in life for the right reasons and with a cheerful heart: "Let each one do just as he has purposed in his heart; not grudgingly or under compulsion; for God loves a cheerful giver" (2 Corinthians 9:7 NASB).

This isn't to say that the goal is for your child to *enjoy* his tasks, jobs, duties, and self-restraints. The mother who says, "You'll eat your peas and like them!" is headed for disappointment. Even Jesus dreaded his most horrible task: dying for our sins. He asked his Father to let the cup of death pass from him (Matthew 26:39). Yet he unwaveringly took on this most important of duties. Kids may need to protest, or they may want to negotiate with you on what you want them to do. At the same time, the goal is that they ultimately are able to accept their burdens willingly and for the right reasons.

The Stages of Motive Development

How do you help your children develop good motivation? God has hardwired several stages of influences through which you will need to guide your children. This is a necessary process. You might notice, as you go through these stages, that your child is at an early level. This isn't necessarily bad—it's simply a marker for the tasks needed to get him to the next stage. No one skips through the stages. The table below summarizes each stage and common mistakes to avoid.

Stage	Mistakes to Avoid
1. Fear of consequences	Angry punishment
2. Immature conscience	Overstrictness or under-strictness
3. Values and ethics	Guilt and shame messages
4. Mature love, mature guilt	Loss of love, overcriticism

Before we explain these stages, understand that children have an enormous task before them in growing up and learning limits; much will be demanded of them by you, reality, and their friends. They need to be rooted and grounded in love (Ephesians 3:17). No one can bear the frustration and pain of responsibility outside of relationship. People can only internalize rules and laws within a grace atmosphere, otherwise they experience rules as something they hate, something that condemns them, or both: The law brings wrath (Romans 4:15).

If you are new to the idea of boundaries and want to start developing them in your child, don't begin with the riot act: "Now hear this! Things are going to change around the Smith household." Make sure you are providing your child with emotional contact, support, and love. Setting boundaries isn't an alternative to loving your child. It is a means of loving her. Be connected to her, reassure her of how much you care. Be with her in her joys and sorrows, even in her anger at and disappointment in you. This contact is what enables her to grow.

Detachment and conditional love are the enemies of this foundation. Detached parents who have difficulty with intimacy may care deeply for their children but are often unable to feel those feelings or communicate them to the child. They love from a distance. If closeness is hard for you, get involved in supportive relationships in which you can learn to be vulnerable and accessible. We can give only what we have received.

Conditional love isn't constant. When a parent's love is conditional, he or she connects to the child only when the child is good. Bad behavior brings withdrawal. A child in this position never feels secure about being loved. He has great difficulty learning basic trust, and he runs the risk of losing all that is important to him if he makes a mistake. No learning can occur if love is conditional.

So love first; set limits second.

1. Fear of Consequences

As you begin setting limits and consequences with your child, she will almost certainly test, protest, and express hatred. No one likes it when the party's over! However, stick with your boundaries, be fair but consistent, and empathize with your child's emotional reactions. She will begin accepting the reality that she isn't God, that Mom and Dad are bigger than she is, and that unacceptable behavior is costly and painful to her. It's a new world. You have her attention.

Nevertheless, children will avoid reality as long as possible. At a baseball game recently, I watched a six-year-old boy talk loudly and incessantly about everything on his mind, bugging all those around him. Mom and Dad, afraid of hurting his feelings, would periodically ask him to please talk more softly. Apparently this was an old scenario for the boy, however; he knew that if he ignored them, his parents would soon give up.

Finally, a fan a couple of rows back walked up to him and said, "Son, you really need to be quiet." Shocked by this firm adult stranger, the child became much more reserved for the rest of the game. Strangely enough, Mom and Dad were not embarrassed, but more empowered to keep better tabs on their child. Getting the child's attention is always the first step.

If all goes reasonably well and you both survive the initial difficulties, your child will develop a healthy fear of consequences. A new thought—*I need to think about what I am preparing to do. What might it cost me?*—replaces the old one—*I am free to do what I want when I want.* This new thought is accompanied by anticipatory anxiety—a little warning light in your child's head that helps him think through how much he wants to do whatever he is contemplating. It is a blessing to your child.

For many parents this occasion represents the first significant victory in child rearing with boundaries. They will begin to think, *This stuff really works!* They have broken into their child's omnipotent self-centered system and introduced the reality that all is not well if he isn't careful. It takes trial and error and lots of effort to find what losses and consequences matter to the child, and it takes lots of stamina to hold the line.

One father told me, "You have to stick to your guns one more time than the child. If he breaks the rule ten thousand times, you have to stay with it only ten thousand and one times, and you'll win." So many parents can remember the day, whether the child was two or sixteen, when they saw a look of doubt and uncertainty pass over their child's face as he realized that his parents were actually going to win the battle by sticking to their boundaries.

Amy, a second grader, had a violent streak. She would throw toys at people when she was angry. The mom set up a system in which, when her daughter threw the toys, she would permanently lose them. The losses were beginning to add up, but Mom didn't know if saying good-bye to cherished toys was registering in Amy's head. Then one day, Amy was once again getting ready to hurl a toy at her. Mom quickly said, "Remember last time?" For the first time in her life, the little girl's arm stopped in its windup, she hesitated, then she dropped the toy. Her mom reported that it was as if her daughter was saying to herself, *I seem to remember something bad happening the last time I did this.* Amy had begun experiencing the crucial association between her actions and her future, what some call a "teachable moment." She was learning about the Law of Sowing and Reaping (Galatians 6:7).

Again, we must stress that this fear of consequences should not be a fear of losing love. Your child needs to know you are constantly and consistently connected and emotionally there with her, no matter what the infraction. She only needs to be concerned about the loss of freedom and the possibility of pain. The message is, "I love you, but you have chosen something difficult for yourself."

This is an early stage of motivation. Some idealistic parents may be disappointed that their child put down the toy because of "Remember last time?" rather than because of "It's wrong" or "I don't want to hurt you." But remember that the law restrains our out-of-control selves enough so that we can slow down and listen to the message of love.

During this stage, avoid setting the limits in anger or in punitiveness. Your child needs to control himself to avoid the consequence. He won't make that connection if he is concerned about avoiding your anger or if he fears some extreme punishment. The focus of learning consequences needs to be that *the child understands that his problem is himself, not an enraged parent.*

Compare these two approaches:

1. "Reggie, you grab those potato chips off the store shelf one more time, and Mom's going to get really angry."
2. "Reggie, you grab those potato chips off the store shelf one more time, and we'll immediately go outside the store for a time-out; then when we get home, you'll be cleaning the kitchen for me for the time I had to waste with you."

In the first scenario, Reggie's problem is an angry mom. His options are to placate her (then get back at her later, or develop a fear of others' anger so that he grows up a boundaryless people pleaser), rebel against her because it's fun to provoke her, or ignore her, knowing he has a couple more chances before she blows up. And if she does blow up and there aren't any consequences, who cares anyway? Many parents have seen their influence on their child's behavior dwindling over time with the anger approach, as the child realizes that the way to deal with parental anger is to tune it out.

In the second scenario, Reggie has to think about his future quality of life: time-outs, kitchen duty, or fun and freedom. The second one helps him see the issue as his behavior, not as an out-of-control mom.

In seeing the issue this way, several things occur for your child: (1) He begins looking at himself rather than blaming others, (2) he develops a sense of control and mastery (he can do something to determine the amount of pain he suffers), (3) he is never without love during this learning process, and (4) he realizes someone bigger and stronger than he—parents, friends, teachers, bosses, the police, the army, or God himself—will always limit him if he refuses to limit himself.

Without these attitudes and character traits built in, your child could remain forever bound in the delusion that whatever he wants, he can have. Helping him with a healthy fear of consequences aligns him with God's reality and makes that reality his friend instead of his nemesis. When your child tells you that he is only doing his chores because he doesn't want to be grounded, praise him. Then begin helping him with the next step.

2. An Immature Conscience

Drew's parents were worried. They had tried to maintain a good balance of love and limits with their three-year-old. But lately he had begun a new behavior they didn't quite understand.

Drew was a "runner"—that is, he ran through the house as fast as he could, knocking over furniture, falling down, and generally being disruptive. His parents worked long and hard with him on this. They talked to Drew about the problem. They gave him the right set of consequences and rewards so that he would walk quietly inside the house. And they began seeing progress. Drew became more careful and deliberate while in the home.

One day Drew came in from playing outside, where he did his running, and he didn't change gears. He began to scoot across the living-room floor. When Dad reminded him of the boundary, Drew said, "Stop, Drew! Bad, Drew!" His parents were worried that he was being harsh with himself.

Children who have begun developing a healthy fear of consequences often begin speaking sharply or critically to themselves, as a harsh parent would, when they misbehave. This applies mostly to kids who are already aware of the connection between their actions and the results.

Drew was involved in a process called *internalization* that occurs all through life. He was internalizing his experiences with significant relationships and taking them into himself. These experiences exist within his mind as emotionally charged memories. Literally, what is outside becomes internal. In a sense, the child "digests" his experiences, and they form part of how he looks at life and reality.

Internalization is a deeply spiritual process by which God instills his life, love, and values in us. As we experience his grace and truth by interacting with him, his Word, and his people, Christ is formed in us (Galatians 4:19). Internalization is the basis of our ability to love, establish self-control, and have a system of morality and ethics. It shapes our conscience and helps us be aware of right and wrong. You may notice, for example, that when you're in a stressful situation or dealing with some problem, a person who has been important to you in that matter may come to mind. You may see his or her face, or be reminded of words that have helped guide you. This is the early stage of internalization, when the influential relationships aren't yet experienced as "me," but as "someone else I value."

For example, Drew listened to his parents' words about the dangers and consequences of running in the house. And as he attended to them, he not only remembered them, but also took on a perception of the very tone of voice they used. He internalized a "parent" instructing him on his behavior.

In Drew's case, he probably didn't internalize the exact words and tones of his parents. They spoke to him firmly but kindly, without the "Bad, Drew" harshness. But, as kids often do, Drew added his own condemning "spin" to the memories.

Children don't internalize absolute reality. Some people think our brain is like a video camera, recording events accurately as they occur. Research indicates, however, that this isn't how memory works. We color our experiences with our opinions, wishes, and fears. This is why outside sources of reality, such as the Bible, are so important. We need places where we can correct our perceptions: "Give me understanding, and I will keep your law" (Psalm 119:34). One of the goals of child rearing with boundaries is for your child to possess an internal sense of love and limits rather than needing a hovering parent, nagging or reminding her to wipe her feet when she comes in the front door.

So, as you lovingly and consistently set and keep limits with your child, she begins to form an internal parent, who does your job for you. The first form this "parent," or early conscience, takes is that of your own words and attitudes, still experienced by the child as someone else, not "me." That's why a younger child like Drew will sometimes talk to himself in the third person. He is responding to all those emotional memories of tangling with you on these responsibility issues.

Sometimes parents can be too strict, authoritarian, or even abusive. This can create a very harsh and immature conscience in a child. Sometimes these children will become either depressed or guilty; at other times they will react against the cruel parent within by acting out the harshness—being mean or sadistic with others. In this case, conscience has gone awry, and the very structure God created to help motivate us now drives us from him, from love, from responsibility, and from each other. If you are concerned about this, consult a wise person who understands childhood issues as to whether you're being too strict.

As conscience is formed and developed, your child is learning to be motivated to love and to be good by internal forces, not just a swat on the behind. He doesn't want to transgress against the internal parent, because it's so much like the real parent. This is good news. You won't always be around to help your child make responsible choices on the playground, at exam time, or in the backseat of a car. Stay consistent, loving, and attentive to your child's changes. If you have a good-enough attachment to your child and he has accepted your boundaries, then your boundaries will become his.

At this stage avoid the two extremes of either being too strict or pulling away the boundaries, as Drew's parents considered doing. We have mentioned the results of overharshness; the fruit of removing boundaries out of guilt or fear of conflict are equally destructive. The child, while initially relieved that Mom and Dad aren't on his case, may become confused about what his limits and structure are. He may act out to provoke an external limit to help him feel safe, or he may develop a sense of entitlement, thinking he is either above the laws or can get around them. Remember to be a parent who wants your child's behavior to correspond with the laws of reality, not your own distortions about reality. Stay in contact with people who know kids, and help your child move to the third stage of motivation.

3. Values and Ethics

After working with the "voices in his head" for a while, the child begins to take all those experiences and put them in more conceptual form. When he disobeys, he doesn't hear so much "Bad, Drew" as "This is a wrong thing to do." This is a sign of increasing structure and maturity in your child. He is beginning to internalize your boundaries more as his own than as an imitation of what you think. We call this the beginning of values and ethics, and this important step is the foundation for much of your child's belief system and attitudes about relationships, morality, and work.

Your child may begin asking many value-laden questions at this point: "Is this a bad word?" or "Is it okay to watch this TV show?" He is wrestling with both understanding your ethics and trying to work out his own. These can be rich times of explaining why you believe what you believe about how people should conduct themselves in the world, and helping your child reach his own conclusions about all this.

This may sound like a pipe dream if you're still working at the level of fear of consequences. But it does work. At the same time, don't think that by this point you are done with setting limits and boundaries with your child. He's still a kid, and in his own way he is attempting to grow up in several dimensions. On one level he is wondering about situational versus absolute ethics, and on another level he is sneaking into the house too late with alcohol on his breath. Be a multitasking parent—that is, meet him where he needs you on both levels.

Avoid the mistake of giving your child guilt and shame messages. Since she now has an operating conscience, which is giving her feedback on her motives for right and wrong, she has a lot to work with daily. She will be especially vulnerable to statements like "I thought you were a Christian, and you still did that" or "I get embarrassed when you don't try hard in school." Kids in this stage easily fall into being "good people" because they want to avoid guilt feelings or shame about themselves. Keep bringing your child back to reality principles like "That goes against what you and we believe."

4. Mature Love, Mature Guilt

As you continue being a source of reality for your child to internalize, he moves and grows beyond the ethical questions of right and wrong to the highest motive: love. As he is more and more connected to others, he begins to think about these abstract issues from a framework of attachment. At the core of his being, your child was created for relationship. Concern for his relationships becomes his most profound motive in life. Jesus summarized all the rules in the Bible into the principle of loving God and people with all your heart (Matthew 22:37). Issues of right and wrong are still very important, but the child understands them from a more relational viewpoint.

You want your child to define love—the greatest motivator—empathically: treating others as we want to be treated (Matthew 7:12). Empathy is the highest form of love; the ability to sense the plight of our condition is what moved God to create, sustain, and redeem us. Outward oriented and relationally based, empathy moves us to caring actions.

Children who are internalizing boundaries need to move beyond "This is right or wrong" to "This hurts others or God." You need to help them with this motive. When they disobey, talk to them about the relational consequences. In other words, "It's not good to make fun of your overweight classmate" becomes "How do you think he feels when kids humiliate him?" Now you are helping your child be an agent of his own internal boundaries, guided and driven by compassion for others.

Avoid either overcriticism or withdrawing love. Being highly critical or pulling away when your child has breached a boundary will often cause him to become compliant rather than loving. Compliant kids are fear based, not love based. They aren't free to choose who and how to love, as they are so driven by avoiding the loss of love or the pain of criticism. Help your child to freely choose and freely love.

A Final Note

In this motivation part of boundary building with your child, don't undervalue any of the three motives for good behavior we have discussed. Your child needs to be concerned about the pain of consequences for irresponsibility, the rights and wrongs of his behavior, and what pain his actions may cause for his friends and God. Be a parent who is subject to these motivations, and create many experiences for your child to internalize and own them for himself.

All parents must grapple with the reality that boundaries cause pain in our children. That is the subject of the next chapter.

— 9 —

Pain Can Be a Gift

The Law of Evaluation

I (Dr. Cloud) was counseling a mom one day about setting limits with her twelve-year-old daughter. Every time I suggested a limit, I would hit a brick wall. Each basic limit or consequence I suggested would not work for one reason or another: Their schedule prohibited Mom from following through; the family would be encumbered; the other siblings would be adversely affected. And on and on. This mom was skilled in telling me why my suggestions wouldn't work.

"Why don't you allow her to miss the party if she can't get her chores done first?" I asked.

"Well, if I did that, we would have to provide a sitter to watch her if we had plans."

"Then let her be in charge of getting and paying for a sitter. She caused the problem, after all."

"Well, I don't think she has the resources to find a sitter. We probably wouldn't like the one she chose anyway."

In the beginning, I thought this mom was being straight with me. But as all my suggestions were dismissed one after the other, I began to feel I wasn't getting the real story. What she was telling me did not ring true, so I stopped our search for the "right" limit for her daughter. Instead, I said to her, "To be honest with you, I don't think you can do this. I don't think you can take the stand with your daughter that needs to be taken. I don't think you can take away the privileges and the money." And then I just looked at her.

At first she began with the "Oh, sure I can" and the "No, really, I know she needs this, and I am committed to it" statements. But I could tell these were defensive answers to my accusation. So I just looked at her and waited.

Then it came. She began sobbing deeply, unable to speak. And then, after gaining control of herself, she finally told the truth: "I just can't stand to hurt her. It's just too painful to see her suffer. If I cut her off, she won't have anything, and I just can't do that to her. She could never make it on her own."

As we talked further, it became apparent that this woman suffered deeply over her daughter's pain. The problem was, however, that she did not understand the pain.

"Why do you think what I am suggesting would be harmful to her?" I asked.

"You've never heard her when I say no to her. It's awful. She cries and withdraws, sometimes for a long time. She feels like I've abandoned her and don't love her anymore."

"Same question. Why do you think it would be harmful to her?"

"I just told you. I have done it, and it hurts her deeply."

"First of all, you have never 'done it,'" I replied. "You have begun and never followed through. And the reason you don't follow through is that you don't know how to evaluate her pain. You think that just because she screams, you are harming her. I don't think you are harming her at all. I think you are helping her, and it just doesn't feel very good."

This insight turned out to be true. This mom did not know how to evaluate her daughter's pain. In short, she did not know the difference between *hurt* and *harm*. The boundaries I was suggesting would definitely hurt her daughter, but they would not harm her. Hurt means that the child, perhaps because of discipline, feels sadness or wounded pride or the loss of something she values; harm means actual injury by wounding her person or, through judgment or attack or abandonment, not providing something she needs. The effective parent must learn this distinction if a child is ever going to develop boundaries.

Pain and Growth

Lesson number one in parenting and life is "Growth involves pain." Lesson number two is "Not all pain produces growth." Learning to tell the difference is the key to having someone stay on the bottom, or grow past where he or she is.

When I played basketball in junior high, our coach had a big banner across the locker room that read, NO PAIN, NO GAIN. This saying became our team's mantra as we conditioned, trained, and practiced, sometimes past the point we thought we could endure.

I had experienced the reality of this phrase before, but I had never understood it quite like this. If I'm not struggling, I'm not getting better at what I have to do. This lesson has served me well for life. If you are independent, you are used to doing things that "hurt" so you can receive something you desire.

For example, as I write this chapter, I am very tired. I'm tired from traveling, and I'm tired of writing. It's a weekend, and I don't like working on the weekend. In addition, I haven't managed my time too well lately, and I'm behind. But as I write, I also know that to continue through the struggle is the only way to get what I desire. I want this book to be published. I want you, the parent, to have it. I want to fulfill this part of what I think God has called me to do. And if the book sells, I can also buy food.

As I write at this late hour, I also groan and gripe about it. Luckily, no one is listening. But what if I called my mother and cried to her about how difficult writing is, how hard it is to make things work in today's world, how cruel life is? And what if she had no boundaries herself, felt "sorry" for my pain, and sent me a check? What if she "compassionately" listened and agreed that I should not push myself so hard? (Don't worry, this is not killing me. But good complainer that I am, I could make it sound that way for a codependent mother.) I could be assuaged out of my suffering enough to just let it go and feel okay about not accomplishing my task.

I can actually remember just such a day when I was in the sixth grade and tried this with my mother. I had had mononucleosis and had missed a month of school. When I came back, I was overwhelmed with the amount of work I had to catch up on. I remember going to my mother and saying, "I do not want to go to school today. It's just too much. I can't take it anymore."

I will never forget what she said. I can see her and hear her words tonight as if I were standing there today: "Sometimes I don't want to go to work either. But I have to go." Then she hugged me and told me to get ready for school.

I was hurting. I was tired. I was in pain. But my mom knew it would not harm me to keep going. She evaluated my pain— the pain of momentary discipline—and encouraged me to keep going. Today, I am thankful for her boundaries. Without them my life would be full of half-done projects and unfulfilled goals. Later, I talked to her about this, and she told me parts of the story I had never heard before.

When I was four years old, a childhood bone disease caused me to lose the use of my left leg for two years. At times I had to use a wheelchair, and at other times I wore restrictive braces and walked on crutches. I was unable to get around much and play with other children.

As you can imagine, this was difficult for my parents to watch. However, when I see home movies, I see an active youngster wheeling through the zoo, going to birthday parties, and hopping around on braces and crutches. For a crippled kid, I did a lot.

I never knew what my parents had to go through to help me become this self-sufficient. The orthopedist told them that they were going to "ruin" me if they did things for me. She told them that they had to let me suffer through learning how to walk on crutches, steer the wheelchair, and explain to others what was wrong with me.

It was extremely painful for my parents to watch me struggle. They already felt sorry for their four-year-old son, who had lost the ability to walk like other children. They wanted to rescue me when I cried about having to wear the brace, or when I was in pain. Instead, they spanked me for trying to walk on my bad leg (something that would have deformed me for life). After she disciplined me, my mom revealed later, she would have to call a friend and cry.

My mother also told me of one day when I was struggling to get up the stairs to church. She overheard someone say, "Can you believe those parents, making him do that? How cruel they are!" But she was able to keep the limits. Another day, my crutch slipped on the marble steps of the post office; I came tumbling down, shaken, bruised, and cut up. But Mom continued to make me go up stairs on my own.

I cried, complained, and tried all of a four-year-old's games to manipulate my mom and dad into not allowing me to suffer the pain of learning self-sufficiency. But they kept their limits, and we made it through.

The end result is that I was soon able to get around and live a reasonably active and normal life with other children, and my leg eventually healed. Today I am grateful for their making me go through pain that hurt me, but did not harm me.

The parent who hears every cry or complaint as the ultimate concern will never develop boundaries and character in the child. When your children cry about homework, chores, or a missed opportunity because they did not do their part, what are you going to do? How you answer this question will have a tremendous effect on the course of your child's life.

Four Rules for Evaluating Pain

Rule # 1: Don't Let Your Child's Pain Control Your Actions

Boundaries with kids begins with parents having good boundaries of their own. Purposeful parents stay in control of *themselves.* If your child is controlling your decisions by protesting your boundaries, you are no longer parenting with purpose.

Terri was having problems with her thirteen-year-old son Josh not doing his homework. We came up with a plan that would require Josh to set aside a certain time each night to do homework. During this hour Josh had to be in his study place with nothing else but his work, and he was not to do anything else but study. Terri had no control over whether or not Josh actually chose to study during that time. What she could control was that he do nothing else during that time but sit with his homework. This was our agreement.

When I saw her the next time, she looked sheepish. She had not lived up to her end of the agreement. (Clue number one that a child will not develop self-control is when the *parent* does not have self-control in enforcing the rules.)

"What happened?" I asked.

"Well, we were all set, and then he got invited to go to a baseball game with his friend. I said no, that his hour was not up yet. But he got so upset, I could not talk him out of it. He seemed so mad and sad."

"So," I said, "that's what he's supposed to do, remember? He hates discipline. So what did you do next?"

"Well, I could see that this requirement was just making him too sad, and I could not stand it. So I let him go."

"What happened the next night?" I asked, already knowing the answer.

"He got upset again. It was a similar situation. He had an opportunity that would have been very sad to miss."

"So let me get this straight. The way you are deciding what is right or not is by how he feels when he is required to do something. If he is upset, then you think it is the wrong thing to do. Is that right?"

"I haven't thought about it that way, but I guess you're right. I just can't stand for him to be sad."

"Then you have got to come to grips with a few important truths. One, your values are being set by the emotional reactions of an immature thirteen-year-old. Your value system's highest guiding principle is whether or not Josh is upset. Two, you don't value one of the most important aspects of child rearing: Frustration is a key ingredient to growth. The child who is never frustrated never develops frustration tolerance. Three, you are teaching him that he is entitled to always be happy and that all he has to do to get others to do what he wants is to cry about it. Are these really your values?"

She grew silent and began to realize what she was doing. To change, she had to commit to an important rule for child rearing:

The child's protest does not define reality, or right from wrong.
Just because your child is in pain does not mean that something bad is happening. Something good may be occurring, such
as his coming to grips with reality for the first time. And this
encounter with reality is never a happy experience. But if you
can empathize with the pain and hold on to the limit, your child
will internalize the limit and ultimately get over the protest.

As we quoted earlier: "No discipline seems pleasant at the
time, but painful. Later on, however, it produces a harvest of
righteousness and peace for those who have been trained by
it" (Hebrews 12:11).

This is a law of the universe. Frustration and painful moments
of discipline help a child learn to delay gratification, one of the
most important character traits a person can have. If you are able
to hold the limit and empathize with the pain, then character (the
"harvest of righteousness") will develop. But if you don't, you
will have the same battle tomorrow: "A hot-tempered man must
pay the penalty; if you rescue him, you will have to do it again"
(Proverbs 19:19). If you rescue your children from their anger
at your boundary, you can plan on more anger at later limits.
Remember, their protest or pain does not determine what is good.

Rule # 2: Keep Your Pain Separate from Your Child's

As Terri and I ultimately discovered, she was trying to make
her own pain go away. When Josh got sad, she got sad. She was
overidentifying with his pain. As a child, she had been let down
many times. She experienced much sadness and loss in her life.
As a result, when Josh was sad, she assumed his sadness was as
bad as her own. She identified with his sadness to a point that
was not real. A child's missing a baseball game does not equal
the sadness she had as a child.

Terri was gradually able to keep her own experience separate
from Josh's and so was able to let him grow. But this was difficult for her, and she needed help to do it. She had some friends
agree to support her at those moments, a strategy that is often
helpful to parents without good boundaries. Remember how my
mother had to go in the other room and cry, calling a friend

for support as she required me to stumble around on crutches while I found my way. You may have to do the same. Keep your own sadness about your children's pain separate from theirs. "Each heart knows its own bitterness, and no one else can share its joy" (Proverbs 14:10). We all must endure our own pain.

Rule # 3: Help Your Child See That Life Is Not About Avoiding Pain, But About Making Good Pain an Ally

Basically, we change when the pain of staying the same becomes greater than the pain of changing. We do our basketball conditioning when the pain of losing becomes greater than the pain of conditioning. We improve our job performance when the pain of losing a job becomes more real than the pain of doing our work. We learn to do our chores when parents make not doing chores more painful than getting them done.

Life is not about avoiding suffering. Life is about learning to suffer well. The child who is taught to avoid pain altogether will encounter much more pain in life than necessary. It is painful to have broken relationships because you do not know how to respect others. It is painful to never meet goals because you are not disciplined. It is painful to have financial difficulties because you can't control your spending.

All these problems come from the tendency to avoid the pain of the momentary struggle, the pain of self-discipline and delaying gratification. If we learn to lose what we want in the moment, to feel sad about not getting our way, and then to adapt to the reality demands of difficult situations, joy and success will follow. Letting a child suffer in the moment teaches this lesson.

Compare what happens later in life to the person who avoids pain and the one who embraces pain (see chart on page 144).

Parents who step in and rescue their children from suffering will be replaced later in life with other codependent people, drugs, alcohol, eating disorders, shopping, or other addictions. They have taught their children that frustration and adversity are not something to face and deal with, requiring change on their part, but something that can be made to go away in the

Situation	Pain Avoider	Pain Embracer
Marital Struggle	• Have an affair • Blame • Go home to mother • Withdraw	• Learn how to love better • Grieve expectations and forgive • Compromise
Job Difficulty	• Quit • Blame management • Turn to alcohol or drugs • Change careers for no good reason and develop a pattern of false starts	• Receive input and criticism • Change behavior • Learn new skills • Respond to authority • Solve problems
Frustration of Achieving Goals	• Procrastinate • Use alcohol, drugs, food, or sex to relieve the frustration • Give up • Get depressed	• Use as an opportunity to learn about self • Gain new knowledge needed to achieve • Face own character weaknesses • Get encouragement from others • Develop spiritually
Emotional Stress, Pain, and Loss	• Deny the issues causing them • Use avoidance mechanisms such as substances or other addictions • Find enabling people who medicate the pain without demanding change	• Accept reality and work through the feelings • Learn positive coping methods of faith, support, grieving, and cognitive change • Deepen spiritual life

immediate moment by using the "mother" or "father" of immediate gratification.

Teach your children that pain can be good. Model facing problems. Model being sad but continuing onward. Empathize with
them about how hard it is to do the right thing, and then still
require it.

I have a friend whose common response to her teenage son's
protest is the same few words: "I know, Tim. Livin's hard. But
I believe you can do it." When this teen becomes a young man,
and the going gets tough, instead of thinking, *How can I get out
of this?* he will hear a voice inside affirm and embrace his struggle: "I know, Tim. Livin's hard. But I believe you can do it."

Rule #4: Make Sure the Pain Is the Pain of Maturing, Not the Pain of Need or Injury

My psychologist friend told of a time when his wife was out
of town for a week, and he was filling the role of Mom and Dad
for his three daughters. About the second or third morning, he
had told his four-year-old several times to get ready for
preschool, and she was dawdling. His frustration was building,
and he was getting angry. Finally, he threatened her with consequences and was starting to show his anger when a question
popped into his head: *What would I do if this were one of my
clients?*

He stepped back for a moment and thought. What he would
do was to look for the reason underlying her behavior. His child
was normally obedient, so he surmised there had to be an
unusual cause for her loitering. Then it hit him, and he asked
her, "You miss your mommy, don't you?" The dam broke. His
daughter began sobbing and ran into his arms. He comforted
her, empathized with her, and said that he missed Mommy, too.

After he had held her a moment and she had calmed down,
she looked up and said, "Daddy, come on, we have to go." She
then got dressed, and things were fine.

Children's behavior often sends a message, and parents need
to evaluate the pain to find out if it is the pain of frustration or
the pain of need or injury. In the case of my friend, the pain

of need was driving his daughter's behavior, and the "limits-only" approach would have disheartened her. The discerning dad evaluated her pain and decided that it was more about missing and needing Mom than it was about defying Dad.

This evaluation is especially important in infancy. Infants protest out of the pain of being hungry and alone more than anything else. Frustration that leads to maturity should be much more in place in the second year of life when discipline and boundaries become more important. The wise mother is able to distinguish between a baby who needs a diaper change, a bottle, or a hug, and one who is overtired or angry about having to go to sleep. Make sure that your small children have had their needs met before you ask them to deal with frustration. *With infants, err on the side of gratification.*

An older child misbehaves not only out of defiance or avoidance of reality, but also for some of these valid reasons:

- Hurt feelings from parents and others
- Anger over feelings of powerlessness in a relationship and not having enough control over oneself
- Trauma, such as loss of a parent or abuse the child may have suffered somewhere
- Medical and physical reasons
- Psychiatric problems, such as attention deficit disorder, depression, or thought disorders
- A recent change in the structure of the family, the schedule, or lifestyle

All these are valid reasons for a child's beginning to misbehave. It is imperative that you rule out these reasons before you assume that your children need reality consequences. These reasons do not rid children of the need to face reality, as the story of my lame leg showed. But the emotional aspects that underlie behavior are just as important as the behavior itself. You may need to take your child to a good pediatrician to make sure that he or she is healthy, or to a child specialist if you suspect something more is going on than a need for boundaries.

Two very important verses in the New Testament give guidance here. The first person you need to rule out as the source of pain is yourself. Listen to the verses:

> Fathers, do not exasperate your children; instead, bring them up in the training and instruction of the Lord (Ephesians 6:4).

> Fathers, do not embitter your children, or they will become discouraged (Colossians 3:21).

Children do not respond well to boundaries if they are exasperated or embittered by their fathers or mothers. Look at yourself to see if you are doing these things:

- Exercising too much control over your children's lives so that they have no power over or choice in their lives
- Disciplining with anger and guilt instead of empathy and consequences
- Not meeting their needs for love, attention, and time
- Not affirming their successes, but only commenting on their failures
- Being too perfectionistic about their performance instead of being pleased with their effort and with the general direction in which they are going

When you evaluate your child's pain, make sure that it is not caused by a real injury or trauma or something other than the real need for discipline and that you have not caused it. Normal parents will cause pain from time to time, but they will see their fault and apologize. It's okay to make mistakes. It is not okay to avoid responsibility for them and blame the child for the behavior that parental mistakes cause.

Consider It All Joy

The following passage from the book of James is one of my favorites: "Consider it pure joy, my brothers, whenever you face trials of many kinds, because you know that the testing of your faith develops perseverance. Perseverance must finish its work so that you may be mature and complete, not lacking anything" (1:2–4).

God does not rescue us from our struggles and the pain of learning discipline and perseverance. In fact, God disciplines those he loves, just as a father disciplines his children (Hebrews 12:5–10). He also says that not disciplining a child is an act of hatred and not love (Proverbs 13:24).

Rubbing precious stones makes them smooth and gleaming. Heat refines gold. Training makes an athlete strong. Delay of gratification and the suffering of study make a student a surgeon. In the same way, struggle refines the character of the child. Waiting for the reward makes a child learn how to perform. Trials and pain teach us the lessons that build the character we will need to negotiate life.

Evaluate your children's pain. If they are in need or injured, run to their rescue. But if they are protesting reality's demands for maturing to the next level, empathize with that struggle, manage it well, but let them go through it to the end. Later, they will thank you.

When children learn to value the pain of life instead of avoid it, they are ready to solve their problems. But what you want is for the child to be proactive in the process. In the next chapter we show how that happens.

— 10 —

Tantrums Needn't Be Forever

The Law of Proactivity

I (Dr. Townsend) live on a street with lots of families with children. One of my favorite after-work, before-dinner pastimes is to gather a bunch of kids and play whiffle ball in the street, where you can draw chalk bases on the asphalt and use plastic bats with foam balls. No windows get broken, and you can have a lot of fun.

During one game, six-year-old Derek struck out. Derek threw the bat down, yelled, "You're all stupid, and I hate you!" and stormed off to his house, where he sat on the steps and glowered at us.

Concerned about Derek's hurt feelings, I left the game, walked over to him, and tried to persuade him to rejoin us. He would have none of it and withdrew even further, turning his body away from us. Finally I gave up and went back to the game, sad that Derek was missing out and that his pals were missing out on him. A few minutes later, Derek got up, walked to the outfield, and resumed play as if nothing had happened.

A couple of evenings later, we threw together another pickup game, and when Derek missed a catch, the same thing happened. He threw a tantrum and left. We played on, adjusting for the lost player, and he again rejoined us when he was ready.

At first I thought, *This is okay. He needs the time to cool down; he's simply taking care of himself.* Then I realized a couple of things. First, Derek was avoiding any problems he encountered in the play. He never had to deal with frustration, failure, or skill building. Learning was preempted by his reactive tantrum.

147

Second, his friends were having to adjust to his immaturity. He had the problem, but they were paying for it. I could tell by their looks and comments that they resented his actions. I felt bad for his future friendship problems.

The next time I saw Derek, I stopped to talk with him. "Derek, I'm sorry you've been having a bad time in the games. It's not easy learning a new sport. But when you leave all the time, it takes you away from fun, and the other kids lose a player, too. So I'm making up a new rule: It's okay to be upset in a game, and we'll help you learn what is hard for you, but it's not okay to leave. If you do, you can't come back for the rest of the game. I hope this will help you hang in with us, because we all really like you and miss you."

Derek acted like he didn't hear me, but I had said things clearly enough.

The next day the kids and I threw together another pickup game. To my dismay, when Derek missed a catch, he threw a tantrum and left, just as he had done so many times before. The rest of us resumed the game. A few minutes later, Derek quietly walked to right field and stood there as usual. I stopped pitching, went over to him, and said, "Sorry, Derek. See you next game." He was furious, and he vowed never to play with us again. He left and went home.

Concerned about Derek's parents' reaction, I called them. They were very supportive of the rule; they too thought Derek's behavior was a problem, but were at a loss about what to do about it.

A few days later, when Derek had another episode, I stuck to the limit.

Finally, the third time, Derek turned around. When he was tagged out at second base, he protested, but this time he quieted down and kept playing. You could see the struggle on his face as he managed his emotions. The kids and I all cheered him for staying with us, and we continued playing. You could tell Derek was proud of himself. He was more in charge of his behavior and his reactions.

Derek illustrates a problem in child rearing and boundaries that exists, at some level, in all of us: the struggle between *reactivity* and *proactivity*, between lashing out in protest or responding maturely to problems. Children need to learn the difference between immature and mature boundaries. Your job is to help them develop the ability to set appropriate boundaries, yet without exploding or being impulsive.

When Kids React

Children don't come by deliberate, thought-out action naturally. They don't accept no easily, and they give up quickly, throwing up their hands in exasperation and walking away from a task that takes sustained effort. They react to stress rather than act upon it. You will often notice a short time lapse between a problem and the child's action, and his action does not usually solve the problem. Derek's reactivity involved honest feelings, but it didn't help him learn to play baseball or get along with other kids any better. Although the child may well be protesting something wrong or bad, his reactions are still immature.

Your child may be adopting the following reactive behaviors:

- *Tantrums.* The smiling, happy child turns into a screaming maniac when you, for example, say no to his desire for a toy at McDonald's. Other customers stare at you, and to keep them from thinking you're abusing your child, you quickly purchase the toy.

- *Oppositionalism.* The child opposes whatever you say or ask. He defies requests to clean his room, pick up after himself, do homework, or come indoors.

- *Whining.* Upon encountering your boundary or some other limitation, the child immediately begins complaining plaintively. There is no reasoning with her, and she can whine for hours.

- *Impulsivity.* When denied something, the child runs away, says hurtful things, or quickly acts out in some way.

When, while shopping in the supermarket, you tell her to come to you, she darts down the next aisle.

* *Fighting and violence.* The child's angry reactions take on physical dimensions. He is easily provoked into school fights. He hurls objects at home. He torments a younger sibling when frustrated.

Several common elements describe reactivity in children. First, children's responses are reactions, not actions—that is, *their behavior is determined by some external influence, not by their values or thoughts.* Children in reaction are in a constant state of protest against something else: a parent's authority, having to delay gratification, or not performing as they would like. They don't take initiative to solve problems, get their needs met, or help meet the needs of others. Rather, they depend on some other motivating force around them.

Second, children's reactions are oppositional—that is, they are opposing something. They are taking a stance *against what they don't like, but not for what they desire or value.* Children's reactive boundaries are in constant protest, like the child who says no to a parent's every suggestion of food to eat in a restaurant. Children use their freedom to disagree as a means to frustrate you. The Bible teaches us not to bite and devour each other in oppositional strife (Galatians 5:15). The word *bite* is a figurative term meaning "to thwart." Oppositionalism is designed to thwart the parent's desire to have control over the child.

Third, *the child's reactive boundaries are not value driven.* A landmark of spiritual and emotional maturity is the ability to base one's decisions on one's values. Our highest value, for example, is to seek God's kingdom (Matthew 6:33). By their very nature, however, children's reactions are not well thought out. Much like the automatic reflex that occurs when the doctor taps your knee with the rubber hammer, the child's actions are not mediated by higher cognitive or value-based aspects of the mind. Many a parent has been shocked by how quickly an angry three-year-old can run out into a street full of traffic as he reacts to a parent's calling him inside. Children act spontaneously and unwisely. If parents don't help them learn self-control, children become like the hotheaded man in the Bible: "A quick-tempered man does foolish things" (Proverbs 14:17).

Reactive Boundaries: Necessary But Insufficient

At this point you may think that reactive boundaries are bad for your child. The reality is, however, that they have their place in his development. Let's take a look at what they are about.

Necessary

What your child really needs is confusing at first glance. Children's reactive boundaries aren't bad; in fact, they are necessary to their survival and growth. Children need to be able to protest what they are against, do not like, or fear. Without it, children are in grave danger of not being able to fend for themselves, much less become self-sufficient or mature.

Protesting the bad is a fundamental boundary for children. They need the ability to "refuse evil and choose good" (Isaiah 7:15 NASB). Kids cannot retain and use the love they receive unless they can shun that which is not good for them. Being able to protest helps the child define herself, keep the good in and the bad out, and develop the ability to take responsibility for her own treasures.

Children need to learn to protest when they are in danger. A child being accosted by bullies on the playground must scream loudly or run for help. A child must also protest if her needs aren't being met. The three-month-old infant screams for Mother when she needs food or comfort.

Not all of the things children protest are bad, however. Life brings many problems and obstacles that aren't evil or dangerous. For example, your child may protest your refusal to buy him a Nintendo 64, or his not getting the teacher he wanted, or your confining him to his room. These are basically problems the child needs to solve. He may need to talk to someone, fight back, negotiate, submit, be patient, or grieve. The child needs to learn this kind of problem solving to learn to become a mature adult.

Protest identifies the problem, but it doesn't solve the problem. This is the difference between reactive and proactive boundaries. While reactive boundaries signal something that needs to be dealt with, proactive boundaries fix something that is broken. Reactive boundaries are often emotionally driven and impulsive and don't involve a great deal of reflection; proactive boundaries are value based, reflective, and solution focused.

In a book about helping kids control their behavior it may seem crazy to support your child's being able to protest. Yet children who do not have this ability to protest—the compliant types—often struggle later in life. Some grow up being dominated and manipulated by more aggressive bosses, spouses, and friends. Unable to say no to the bad, they are taken advantage of. Others develop reactive boundaries in adult life and go through severely tumultuous periods when, at age thirty-five, they have a two-year-old's tantrums. God designed us to go through stages of growth. These stages can't be skipped over (1 John 2:12–14). And if we navigate them more or less correctly, they lead to freedom and maturity.

When my younger son, Benny, was eight or ten months old, I was feeding him strained broccoli with a spoon. I had just come home from work and hadn't taken off my blazer yet. Little did I know that Benny wasn't interested in broccoli. But in his own way, he informed me of that reality.

Benny didn't let me know about his aversion to broccoli proactively. He didn't pipe up and say, "Dad, I don't like broccoli. Can we negotiate something here? Can we work out my getting the basic nutrients I need in another food other than broccoli?" He did what many babies do with broccoli: He spit it out. My blazer took the brunt of his reactive boundary. This experience—and many others—helped Benny take charge of his feelings, experiences, and treasures.

Children have reactive boundaries for many reasons. They feel powerless and helpless, so they react. They have a young, immature character, so they can't delay gratification and think through conflicts very well yet. They aren't able to observe themselves and others, so they quickly deal with the frustration, no matter what the consequences.

Reactive boundaries lead to mature, loving boundaries and actions through a sequence of abilities and skills:

- The child is born into fear and helplessness. She is afraid of being hurt, losing love, or dying. She has little ability to care for and protect herself.
- The child becomes compliant out of fear. Because she fears the effects of resisting, she allows unwanted things, such as not having all her desires met, frustration, her parents' absence, even abuse.
- If she is loved enough to feel safe with her feelings, she begins to safely experience her rage at what she doesn't like or want.
- She sets her reactive boundaries and protests with tears, tantrums, or acting out.
- These boundaries allow her to define herself and identify the problems that need solving. She becomes free to say no as well as yes.
- With the support and structure of her parents, the child develops proactive boundaries, which become based on higher and higher levels of motivation (see chapter 6), culminating in godly altruism—loving God and others (Matthew 22:37–40). She has no need to have tantrums, as she doesn't feel helpless and controlled. She is in control of herself.

Insufficient

As we see in the above sequence, reactive boundaries are insufficient for a successful adult life. They protect and help separate your child from bad things, but reactivity is a state, not an identity.

One reason reactive boundaries are insufficient is that children who never move beyond reactive boundaries develop a victim identity. As adults they feel controlled and put upon by external forces, such as spouses, bosses, the government, or God. They don't see themselves as having any choices, so they remain helpless. They look at most of their struggles in life as coming from the outside, not from inside themselves. Thus, they are forever prohibited from improving their lives because *no problem that originates outside of us is really solvable.* Most of our pain comes from either our own mixed-up attitudes or our responses to mixed-up others. When we understand this, we become free to choose.

The other reason that reactive boundaries are insufficient is that children need to grow up to be defined by more than what they hate. Reactive boundaries only help kids with what they are against. Children who remain in the reactive phase have difficulty making and keeping friends, getting along with authorities, attaining goals, and finding talents, interests, and passions. They are so invested in the "against," they aren't able to develop the "for." Derek, for example, had problems making friends because he had developed a reputation for being against teamwork, rules, and cooperation.

If your child is compliant and quiet about everything, there may be a problem. Like Benny, he may be overdue for some broccoli-purging! And it is better that it come now rather than in his marriage. Encourage your child to think for himself, disagree, and talk about his feelings while accepting your authority. Reactivity helps your child seek and find his boundaries. But once he has found them, once he knows what he doesn't like, he isn't free to indulge his feelings by seeking revenge, avoiding dealing with them, or getting out of his responsibilities.

Proactive Boundaries

I have coached youth soccer for the last few fall seasons. On the first day of practice we meet our kids and start working on skills and strategies. Within minutes I can tell which kids have reactive boundaries and which have proactive ones. On the one hand, those with reactive boundaries don't like instruction, get into poking fights with each other, irritate quickly, and get tired of drills they don't do well at immediately. You hope they will improve over the season. Those with proactive boundaries, on the other hand, pay attention, make mistakes and learn from them, and speak up if they don't like something or if they need something. A boy with reactive boundaries, for example, will get tired and yell that the coach is mean because he is working them too hard. One with proactive boundaries will ask the coach for a break or some water.

Proactive boundaries come from the maturing of a child's reactive boundaries. Here's what proactive boundaries look like, and here are some ways to help your children develop them.

Proactive boundaries go beyond problem identification to problem solving. Your child needs to know that in protesting, she has only identified the problem, not solved it. A tantrum doesn't solve anything. She needs to use these feelings to motivate her to action, to address the issue at hand. She should think about her responses and choose the best one available.

To help your child with this task, use the reactive boundaries she experiences. Empathize with her anger and frustration, but let her know that the only way to end the problem is for her to solve it herself. Say something like, "I know you get mad when you have to turn off the TV and start your homework. Work isn't as fun as play. But if you fight me over the TV, you'll be choosing to be without it for a week, and I don't think you want that. So, is there a way you can just let me know you're disappointed in leaving the TV and still do what I say?" After a few trials, she should be convinced by experience that you're serious about your own boundary. Tell her she can let you know appropriately that she hates homework. At this point the child will often settle in to a standard "Oh, Mom, I hate homework" as she gets up from the couch and picks up her pencil.

Remember that your job isn't to make her enjoy leaving the TV and doing homework; it's to encourage her to take responsibility to do the right thing. She needs her own opinions and feelings so that she can develop her own identity. Some parents and teachers demand, "Do what I want and like it!" They insist that the child conform both in behavior *and* attitude. These people dismiss the child's experience and either exasperate or discourage her (Ephesians 6:4; Colossians 3:21).

Proactive boundaries encompass both what the child is for and against. While reactive boundaries help children identify what is "not me" and what they don't like, maturity is much more than

this. Children need to know both what they are and what they
are not, what they love and what they hate. When they develop
their loves, such as close friendships, hobbies, tasks, and talents,
they are being driven and motivated by what is good and right.
God defines himself by both what he hates (Proverbs 6:16–19)
and what he loves (Micah 6:8).

Help your child develop the "for" aspects of proactive boundaries. A situation in which there has been an issue over reactive boundaries is often a good learning ground. As the child feels
safe protesting and expressing his dislikes, he can also be more
open to listening to his parent's teaching. Tell your child, "I
understand that you are angry about not being able to go out
with your friends tonight. But we believe it's important for you
to spend a certain amount of time with the family and doing your
homework. We aren't saying no just to be mean."

In one family I know, seven-year-old Taylor was going through
a titanic power struggle with his mother. He fought any "do"
or "don't" she said. His reactive boundaries were clear and consistent. Finally his mom went to his bedroom to talk to him. As
she opened the door, a cup perched on the top of the door tipped
over, covering her from head to toe with milk.

Any parent would have blown up at her child. Instead, Taylor's mom said, her face dripping with milk, "Son, this is really
serious. I'm going to have to take some time to figure out what
will be happening to you. I'll let you know." The next few hours
were excruciating for Taylor as he waited in limbo. By that time
the mom had called her husband and worked out a plan. The
plan included restrictions on Taylor's time—such as no TV, limited outdoor time, and limited friend time—and consequences—such as shampooing the carpet and learning how to
use a washing machine to clean Mom's clothes.

Another development helped Taylor's reactive boundaries
move to the proactive level. To avoid feeling like the bad guy,
he joked with his dad about the incident, saying, "Dad, wasn't
that kind of funny?"

His dad responded with a straight face, "No, it was really mean,
Son. You went too far with your anger. It was hard on your mom."

"But I saw it on a show, and it was a good trick."

"Taylor," his dad said firmly but not harshly, "I really don't want to talk about any part of this behavior being funny. It just wasn't."

A few hours later, the boy's mother overheard Taylor saying to his little sister, "No, Kelly, don't laugh! The milk trick wasn't funny. It hurts people." Taylor's boundary with Kelly was far different from the one he had with Mom. It was love based and deliberate. Through some tough consequences with Mom and some verbal boundaries about reality with Dad, Taylor was metabolizing his reactive boundaries and becoming more empathically based. He was developing a concern for the feelings of others.

This change often happens after you empathize with a reactive boundary, but don't give in to it. Your child will take in your loving boundary and soften his own harsh one. Children will sometimes go through a "good as gold" season after an incident like this. They will do unasked-for favors for others or obey without a lot of resistance. If you have withdrawn from or attacked the child, this season may be an attempt to regain connection with you. But if you are maintaining your attachment to your child, this behavior may occur because your child has met your limit, feels less out of control and fearful of his own impulses, and feels safe. This then leads to a sense of gratitude and warmth toward his family. Again, that is the nature of proactive boundaries.

Proactive boundaries mean others can't control the child. Children who have reactive boundaries and who live in protest are still dependent on other people. Like a pinball, they bounce from parents to siblings to friends, complaining about their poor treatment at the hands of others. Their feelings and actions are motivated by what others do or don't do to them. Children with proactive boundaries, however, aren't driven by the control of others. They have what is called an internal locus of control; that is, how they view life, their decisions and responses to the environment, are all dictated by their own internal values and realities.

You can help your child attain this important aspect of mature boundaries. When he is in his reactive "protest mode," remember to validate his feelings yet still hold to your limit or consequence. Then say, "You know, the more you fight me, the less time you have for things you like to do. Then it will be time for bed. I'm willing to stop the argument if you are, then you can go play. What do you think?" If the child isn't ready to stop, he thinks you don't mean what you say. Don't give in, and don't keep arguing. Stick to your guns. Eventually he should realize that *as long as he is giving up all this time reacting to you, you are in control of his precious time.* Having to go to bed with less playtime will help him understand the biblical principle of time management: Make the most of every opportunity (Ephesians 5:16).

Often the "sensitive child" struggles with this part of boundary growth. He is easily hurt by the unkindness of others toward him, real or perceived. He seeks comfort from his mother, who does her best to reassure him, then he goes out and gets hurt again. When he is old enough to go to school, the tougher kids smell his scent and go for the kill. He gets a reputation as an easy mark.

The sensitive child is often highly dependent on others' reactions instead of his own values. All is right in the world if everyone is kind to him and agrees with him. He has an infantile wish for total closeness with all, with no separateness or conflict. If your child has this tendency, you need to help him use proactive boundaries to gain more internal control and free him from his misery.

My friend Jan had a daughter with this problem. Nine-year-old Brittany constantly came home crying because others were mean to her. Jan would check it out, and sometimes people were being mean, but sometimes they were just doing what kids do. After finding that lots of reassurance and encouragement to work out the problems with Brittany's friends wasn't solving the issue, Jan and I talked. We found out that Jan was unknowingly operating, not as the solution to Brittany's struggle, but as the problem.

Jan would listen attentively to Brittany talk for hours on end about every little thought, feeling, or action she experienced. However long it took for Brittany to talk through her day, Jan would listen patiently. Although it was wearing on her, Jan figured Brittany simply needed more connection time. But Brittany needed much more time processing her feelings with Mom than did either her sister or her brother.

Jan's indulgence was making Brittany quite dependent on her mother's understanding. Brittany didn't feel confident and able to take care of herself, as Jan was always there. Then, when her friends would squabble with her, Brittany had no internal resources to fall back on. She would feel unloved and helpless. She felt controlled by her friends. And unknowingly, she was controlling Jan, who was not keeping boundaries with her daughter. Brittany was not controlling what was hers (her relationships with friends) and was controlling what wasn't hers (Jan's time). So Brittany stayed reactive.

Realizing all this, Jan sat down with her daughter and explained, "Honey, I love you, and I love our time together. But I just don't have enough time for every single one of your thoughts and feelings. And I want you to take responsibility for your own emotions, too. I know you can think for yourself and handle them. So from now on, I will have twenty minutes at night for share time for you, then that will be all, unless there's a really bad problem that can't wait. So you be sure to tell me the most important things you want me to know."

Of course, this wasn't all the time Jan gave to Brittany, but it was the only really structured time. Brittany didn't like it and tested the boundary, but Jan stuck to it. Jan saw her gradually develop more confidence in her friendships and fewer tears. Brittany was becoming more proactive in taking care of herself. A couple of times, the little girl even forgot her share time with Mom because she was busy doing something else. Brittany was out of the control of other people, as was her mother. Remember, "each one should carry his own load" (Galatians 6:5). There is wisdom in the old saying, *If you want to fix the child, fix the parent.*

Proactive boundaries are not about revenge and fairness, but about responsibility. Reactive boundaries operate under the law "an eye for an eye." If one child shoves another, the other shoves back. This payment in kind is motivated by justice and revenge. Proactive boundaries, however, are more concerned with higher motives, such as responsibility, righteousness, and love for others.

As the New Testament teaches, "Do not repay anyone evil for evil" (Romans 12:17). Your child should be about the business of restraining evil in himself and others, not exacting revenge for it. This work of paying for evil, thereby removing the need for revenge, was already finished on the cross (1 Peter 2:24). This also includes demands for fairness and justice.

We support kids' being able to take care of themselves. Self-defense classes, for example, can help a child learn to defend himself and have confidence in his ability to function with other kids. However, we do not support the idea that when the child is angry, he should get into a fight. This confuses reactive with proactive boundaries.

Reactive boundaries demand retribution. Many combative adults, who today can't hold a job or a marriage without enormous power struggles, never outgrew their reactive stances as children. They can't let go of a grievance or offense and simply move on. Proactive boundaries function very differently. The child with proactive boundaries doesn't allow himself to be taken advantage of or harmed, but he isn't a crusader against every bully on the playground. A good way to look at the difference is this: *With reactive boundaries, you fight the friend who constantly bugs you. With proactive boundaries, you decide you don't need that kind of a friend.*

Demands for fairness are a related problem for parents. When, for example, your child reacts to some problem with, "It's not fair!" you will either feel guilty about not being perfectly fair or ally with the child against a bad friend or teacher. This keeps the child in a reactive phase. It encourages her to feel like a victim and to somehow expect fairness in the world. Instead, tell your child, "You're right—lots of things aren't fair. And it's not fair that I let you off the hook sometimes when you deserve punishment. Your needs are very important to me, but perfect fairness isn't. In this family, as long as you're okay, that's fair enough for you." This helps the child focus on getting his needs met, not judging the world for not being fair to him.

The Skills of Proactive Boundaries

Proactive boundaries are learned over time, developed as fine gold from the ore of reactive boundaries. You need to teach your child several skills that, when joined with her protest stance, will enable her to be a self-controlled, value-based person. Some of them are listed below. Approach these to the extent that you have these skills. If you don't have them, let your child know it and work on them together.

Timing is important here. Don't go over these skills while you are still in the war. Wait until your child is in a teachable place, generally after several failed assaults on your boundaries.

- **Pausing instead of reacting.** When your child reacts instantly in protest, make him repeat the desired action several times, talking him through it each time, until he sees he doesn't have to react. The child who angrily slams the door needs to see that he is capable of twenty or thirty soft closes, even when he is mad.
- **Observation.** Help your child become a student of himself. Go over the incident, helping him see other realities besides his frustration.
- **Perspective.** Your child needs your input on her anger and rage. She thinks her feelings are ultimate truth. Help her look at her feelings as feelings: They will go away. They don't always show us absolute reality. Others' feelings are important, too.
- **Problem solving.** Help your child see other alternatives to solving his problem or getting his need met. "If Bobby won't play with you, how about trying Billy?"
- **Reality.** Help your child compromise and negotiate results that aren't black and white. She needs to know her needs won't get met perfectly, but good enough is good enough. She may not have the lead in the school play, for example, but her part is a good part.
- **Initiative.** Your child needs to understand that until she is proactive with the problem, she will be forever reacting to the same problem, with no solution. Listen to talk

radio: Why are people griping about the same old thing
every day? Don't reinforce the griping; push her to be a
solver.

- **Other people.** If you have done your best and you don't
  know what to do, ask someone you trust. Don't be a Lone
  Ranger Mom or Dad.

Conclusion

Parents need to worry about all sorts of things. You need to
worry if your child has never had a tantrum. But you need to
worry if your child has too many tantrums and is stuck in a reactive stage. From a loving, firm position, you can help your child
mature his reactive boundaries into love-and-reality-based proactive boundaries, helping him take control of his life, character,
and morality: "Blessed is the man who does not walk in the counsel of the wicked or stand in the way of sinners or sit in the seat
of mockers" (Psalm 1:1).

If there is anything that destroys honesty and self-control in
your child, it is gossip, or what psychologists call triangulation.
In the next chapter you will learn about helping him expose his
boundaries in the light of relationship.

— 11 —

I Am Happier When I Am Thankful

The Law of Envy

"B ut Susie has one!"
"I'm bored."
"I'm tired of this toy. I want that one."
"That's not fair. Joey gets to!"
If any of these statements sound familiar, you have dealt with envy. If you have a child, you have dealt with envy. Envy is the basest human emotion, and to some degree, all humans envy. But as you have noticed, not all humans possess the *same* degree of envy, nor does it rule everyone's life. Look at the adults around you, and see if you can recognize how envy plays a role in some of the more unhappy people you know. Envious people

- Long for more and more material possessions
- Tire of their spouse and want one more exciting
- Are unable to feel content and enjoy the things they have
- Need to keep up with the Joneses
- Overvalue position, power, status, and money
- Are continually dissatisfied with their job or career
- Have a critical attitude toward people who have power, status, talents, or things
- Envy people who are in a higher class than they are
- Continually feel entitled to special treatment and have the world see them as "special"
- Feel they are above criticism or being questioned

The saddest aspect of envy, though, is the emptiness envious people continually feel. Nothing is good enough, nothing fulfills them. No matter what they achieve or receive, something is wrong with it, and contentment is forever missing in their lives.

Translated back to children, envy is the perpetual "wanting more." Normal to some degree, this problem should be disappearing as a child grows in accepting boundaries. The purpose of this chapter is to teach you how to transform normal childhood envy into acceptance, gratitude, and contentment.

Entitlement Versus Gratitude

Pointing to the one character trait that causes more misery in people's lives than any other would be difficult. But it would not be tough to come up with a list of finalists! Certainly, one of the top three or four destructive traits would be having a feeling of entitlement. Entitlement is when someone feels as if people owe him things or special treatment simply because he exists.

People with this character trait feel entitled to privileges, special treatment, things other people have, respect, love, or whatever else they want. And when they do not get what they want, they feel that the one who is not giving it to them is "wrong." They protest as if they were a victim of bad treatment from the other person, organization, God, or whoever has the desired object. They carry around a feeling of "you should," and they are always demanding something from someone.

In adulthood these people often feel entitled in their jobs to promotions, a pay increase, or special privileges they have not earned. In marriage, they criticize their spouses for not doing enough for them or not giving in to the things they feel they need. After a while, employers and spouses tire of the complaining and the blame—and eventually the person.

Children first feel entitled to be in control. They want what they want when they want it, and they protest when they don't get it. Early in life, babies do need immediate attention and care. But as they receive this and get a bit older, feeling entitled and not adapting to the needs of reality and others in the family or on the playground or in school becomes an obnoxious trait.

Next, children feel they are entitled not to suffer, to work, or to adapt to rules and boundaries.

Later, children feel entitled to what others have. Hence, the familiar refrain "But Susie gets to go—I should, too" or "But Susie has one—why can't I?" "If someone else has it, I should have it too" is the feeling they carry around and try to enforce. It is not unusual to see a child playing happily with a toy, seemingly enjoying herself, until she sees something another child has. All of a sudden, that toy is more desirable. Children envy what another has, and what they have becomes no good at all. And then they protest if they can't have that other thing. They feel entitled to it.

The opposite of envy and entitlement is gratitude. Gratitude comes from the feeling of freely receiving things, not because we deserve them, but because someone has graced us with them. We feel a thankfulness grounded in love, and we cherish what we have received. But more important, we feel that "we are so fortunate to have what we have." This contrasts sharply with the entitled and envious feeling of "we are being cheated for having only what we have." The grateful person is happy and filled with joy; the envious person is miserable and filled with resentment. There are not many things worse than being around an envious and entitled person; there are few things better than being around thankful and grateful people.

The two states—envious and grateful—have little to do with what a person actually receives. They have more to do with the character of the person. If you give something to entitled, envious people, it profits them or you nothing. They just feel that you have finally paid your debt to them. If you give to grateful people, they feel overwhelmed with how fortunate they are and how good you are. Parents need to help children work through their feelings of entitlement and envy and move to a position of gratitude.

The Problem of Two Mommies and Two Daddies

When children come into the world, they are confused about the nature of their relationships. They do not think they are dealing with one person. In their minds, there are two mommies, not one. Or two daddies, not one. There is the good mommy or daddy and the bad one. The good one is the one who gratifies them. When they are hungry or needy, they protest, and the good mommy comes and relieves their stress. When they are gratified, they see this mommy as "good." But if something they want is not forthcoming and Mommy frustrates their wish, she is seen as the "bad" mommy. You may even remember this literally happening. It is not unusual for a child to hear no and say, "Bad Mommy." This split is universal.

Some adults have still not resolved this problem. If you do what they want, they are very loving and see you as a good person. But if you say no to them, they see you as bad for not giving them what they wanted. A great sin indeed! Then when you gratify them, you are seen as good all over again.

The other side of this is what goes on inside children. When they are getting what they want, they see themselves as *entitled* to what they are receiving; when they are being frustrated, they see themselves as *victims* of the "bad mom." So not only do they see two mommies, but they also experience two selves as well: the entitled self and the deprived self. You can probably remember seeing this in very young children. When happy, they are very happy, and when angry or sad, they are very angry or sad.

But as children experience both having their needs met and being frustrated with limits, they slowly merge the two images of themselves and others. They slowly realize a few extremely important things:

1. My needs are consistently responded to.
2. Not all my needs and wants are gratified.
3. The same person is both giving to me at some times and depriving me at other times—the one I love is the one I hate.
4. I am fortunate at times, and at other times I have to deal with being frustrated.

As this combination of gratification and frustration occurs a few million times, children gain a secure sense of the world's being "not perfect" in gratifying them all the time, but "good enough" in giving them what they need. They slowly give up their wish for the "all-good other" who is going to meet all their needs perfectly and learn to love the one who both loves them and frustrates them. And they decide people are not perfect, but good enough. Children endure enough frustration to become grateful for what they receive as they find out they are not entitled to everything they want.

To accomplish this task, children need two important things from you: *gratification* and *frustration*. Children who are never gratified are in a constant state of need, and they will never feel grateful because they literally have not gotten enough. This is the danger of parenting systems that overemphasize depriving the child early in life for fear that the child will control the home. *Children must have their needs met to develop trust and gratitude.* As the Bible says about us and our Father in heaven, "We love because he first loved us" (1 John 4:19). We need to be given to first.

But children who are never frustrated never understand that they are not the center of the universe, that they are not owed whatever they want, and that others do not exist only for their needs. The balance of gratification and frustration tempers the extremes of neediness and entitlement. As the Rolling Stones put it in their album *Let It Bleed,* "You can't always get what you want. But if you try sometimes, you just might find, you get what you need." The child who experiences frustration gives up the view that he's entitled to everything he wants and that others should perform for him. In addition, he doesn't see himself as a victim when he's deprived, nor does he see others as bad when they do not do what he wants. He develops a balanced view of himself and others.

Giving, Limiting, and Containing

To give your child a balanced sense of themselves and others, you must gratify needs and some wants, and frustrate others. The three skills necessary to do this are giving, limiting, and containing.

Giving

Giving is the gratification of needs and wants. The most important gratification is the one for love, connection, and care. This is the cry of the infant when he is hungry and alone. He must be attended to, nurtured, and connected with. As he takes in food and care, warmth and safety, the building blocks of gratitude are being formed. Much of the envy that adults feel is a very deep longing for needs to be gratified, to be cared about at a deep level.

As they get a little older, children need to be comforted. Their fears need soothing. Their feelings need understanding. Their anxiety about going to the next step needs encouragement. Life is getting bigger, and they need to know that they are not traveling alone. Their screams of fear need to be gratified with reassurance.

Older yet, children's need for freedom, space, and some control and choices has to be gratified. This is the building block of independence. Children want some choices, and they should have some. They want some space, and they should have some. They want some control, and they should have some of this, too. Learning to want what they want and to ask for what they want are important skills they will need in life. They need to have this need (for freedom, space, some control, and choices) satisfied to know that it's good, that it works, and that the world wants to help (that is, the world will help try to satisfy the need).

Then children will want to have things, activities, and resources, such as money and opportunities, to learn and explore their skills and talents. They need to have those needs gratified. As they get older, they certainly need to have a part in earning and supplying some of these resources, but their skills and talents should not be frustrated.

Their further drives for independence and freedom mature, and they should be gratified as well. As they exercise responsibility and good choices, they need to learn that they will be rewarded as the Bible teaches: "He who is faithful in little will be given more" (see Matthew 25:21, 23).

Children need to experience gratification in all these areas. As they get older and older, they have an increasing responsibility in securing and using these gifts of money, opportunity, and talents. But they need to know that the world is a place where they can receive things and fulfill their talents and dreams. At the same time, they are learning that they must be responsible and wise. As Solomon said to those who are young, "Follow the ways of your heart and whatever your eyes see, but know that for all these things God will bring you to judgment" (Ecclesiastes 11:9). In the same way, the Hebrew word translated "weaned" literally means "to have dealt bountifully with." Children need to receive "bountifully" before they are "weaned" for life. Give to them, meet their needs for love and affection, and give them opportunities to grow and the equipment they need to carry out their life tasks.

Limiting

Limiting is making sure children do not get too much or do not get inappropriate things. Limiting is making sure, as we have said earlier, that their wish to be in control of everything is not gratified. In addition, limiting is disciplining and managing their choices and consequences. It has to do with the way you live out the word *no* and make it reality.

In infancy, setting limits has a very small role. Infants are already limited by their physical existence. They need a lot, and they can't ask for it because they can't talk; they can't get it for themselves because they can't walk. Limits play a role in infancy when an infant has had all that she needs and now just has to go to sleep. The wise mother knows the fussy cry versus the cry of need. Fussy gives way to sleep. If a need is frustrated and gives way to sleep, problems will develop—which is why during infancy we always recommend erring on the side of gratification.

In toddlerhood, however, limits become the order of the day. Toddlers are more and more mobile, and they want more and more control. They learn limits for the first time as the word *no* truly begins to have meaning. They find that they are not entitled to everything they want. They reach, and hear no for the first time. They are learning they are not in control. They want you to stay with them, and yet you go out for the evening. They are learning that they are not entitled to whatever their hearts desire. They are learning the limits of their wish to be in control. They want candy, and they can't have it. Sometimes they can have a legitimate need, yet they don't get that need met simply on the grounds that they want it. They may have to do something to get it, such as asking and using words instead of whining or manipulating.

Later on in childhood, they want toys that they cannot have. They want the newest and the best, when the one they have will do. (Think how that translates into credit card spending later!) When they hear no and you keep your stand, they are learning that the world is not going to just give them whatever they want.

Sometimes children learn that goal and desire can be a good thing, but you still do not give them what they want. *They have to earn it.* Parents who merely give children whatever they want and do not teach them how to work for things they desire are reinforcing entitlement in a major way.

In addition, just because their brother or sister has something, or a friend has it, does not mean that they will get it. Parents often hear the protest of "That's not fair!" when they don't get what others get. We say, "So what?" It will be like that the rest of their lives. Better to learn it now.

In the teen years, the limits are fewer, but just as important. Teens need more and more freedom and choices and opportunities to be responsible, but they also need clear and enforced limits to obey. The teen years are your last chance to show your children they are not in control of the universe. If they do not get this idea from you, they will get it from the law; it is better to get it from Mom and Dad. Curfews, financial limits, and obeying the boundaries of what choices are allowed all give opportunities to limit a teen's wish to be in control of the universe and above all laws.

Much attitude adjustment is needed during the teen years. Teens are gradually taking on the guardian and manager role for themselves (see chapter 1), and when they begin to taste this freedom, sometimes it is not pretty. They can be grandiose, condescending, and mean. Good limits on how you allow them to treat you shows them that they are not entitled to treat people any way they want.

Throughout the developmental spectrum, limiting your children is important in overcoming envy and entitlement. You must not reinforce their feeling that they are entitled to have whatever they want, to do whatever they want, or to treat people however they wish. If you balance good limits with gratification, they will find out they do not own the world.

Here are some thoughts on the role of limiting:

- Limits begin in infancy when, having had all their needs met, infants experience separateness at times.
- Limits begin to kick in formally in toddlerhood as children learn they are not the boss, and limits continue through the teen years.
- Limits teach children that they are not entitled to whatever they want, even though their wants may be good. They have to work to achieve what they want; desire is not enough.
- Limits teach children that life is not fair, if they define fair as equal. They will never have the same as everyone else. Some will have more, some will have less than they will.
- Limits help children learn that their feelings are not ultimate reality.
- Limits are important in bringing out children's protest so parents can empathize with their children and contain their feelings while keeping the limit.
- Limits and discipline show children their badness, so they do not think they are innocent victims of the universe.
- Limits instill confidence because children find they can survive the deprivation of some of their wants and learn to meet some of their own needs.
- Limits give them a structure for how to treat others. Children who have experienced loving limits can set them.
- Limits help them experience grieving for what they cannot control, so they can let it go and resolve it.

Do not rob your children of limits. Otherwise, they will have the lifelong burden of thinking they are God. That is a role at which they are sure to fail.

Containing

Containing is helping a child to work through feelings about a limit and to internalize that limit as character. *Limits in and of themselves are too brutal for humans to use.* As the Bible says, they exist in hostility against us when they are present without grace (Ephesians 2:14–15). Limits seem mean, adversarial, cold. None of us can enforce them very well without love.

So, containing adds love, understanding, and structure to limits in order that the child can internalize them. When a child encounters a limit, she reacts with anger. We all react with rebellion and rage when we first encounter no. We perceive limits as our enemy. So we protest in some fashion.

If the limit is removed because of our protest, we learn that we are bigger than the limit. It would have been better if no limit had been given at all, because we tried on our God role and won. Our thinking that we are in control was reinforced. (It is better not to have any limit at all than to have a limit you are not going to enforce.)

If the limit stays, the child must be won over to its side. The staying power of the limit breaks the grandiosity of the child— a severe wound. Someone must turn that rage into sadness, grief, and resolution. You do this with comfort, care, empathy, and connection. You keep the limit while giving the child empathy:

- "I know, honey, it's hard."
- "I agree, it's not fair."
- "I hate it, too, when I don't get to do what I want."
- "I understand. No, you still can't go."
- "Livin's hard, huh?"

These empathic statements show the child that someone is on his side even while the limit seems so against him. Then, through a process, he is able to use the limit to learn whatever he needs to learn; the love helps him to internalize the limit.

Many parents at this point have difficulty letting their children be hurt and angry, using empathy as their only antidote. Avoid statements designed to make you feel better:

- "This is going to hurt me more than it hurts you." (Now the child has not only a parent who won't let her do something, but one who does not understand.)
- "I am doing this because I love you, and you will thank me for it later." (The child cares only about the present.)

- "It's not that bad. Think of all the good things you have gotten to do lately."
- "It will only last a little while."
- "Stop crying, or I'll give you something to cry about."

What the child needs most at this moment is empathy and understanding that life has dealt her a difficult blow. This combining of love and limits will turn into internal limits and structure and will be a blow to her entitlement. Remember, your children are losing more than what they wanted. They are losing their entire view of life; they are learning that they are not in control. Expect them to hate this for a little while.

Courage to Be Hated

The parent who cannot tolerate being hated will not be able to provide the reality the child needs to overcome feeling entitled. Love and limits are the most important qualities for a parent. The ability to tolerate being hated and seen as "bad" is a parent's next most important quality. God, as the ultimate parent, is able to do what is right and to take a stand, no matter what anyone thinks of him. He loves, but he has his standards and keeps them, even when we do not like it. If he did not, the universe would be in trouble. One of the great lessons of the book of Job is that no matter what Job thought of God, God did not strike back at him or cease to be God. The same is true for a parent. You need to be able to contain the protest, stay connected, not strike back, and remain the parent.

When "Thank You" Does Not Come

"Thank you" needs to be taught early. "What do you say, honey?" is a common parental question when a child receives something. Children who are being loved and disciplined usually develop gratitude naturally because of the following factors:

- Their entitlement is being limited with discipline.
- Discipline for their rebellion and trespasses is teaching them that they are not innocent victims.
- They are having to say, "I'm sorry."

- They are being humbled.
- Parents are modeling it in saying "thank you" to the child and to each other.

Expressing gratitude is a very important aspect of development. If it is not appearing, it needs to be addressed. A child who is not expressing thanks needs to be talked to and limited. He is taking things for granted. Let him know that this is not appreciated by others. Don't do this to impose guilt, but with the same formula of sharing your feelings *and* your limits on giving:

- "When you're bossy with me, you'll get less."
- "When you say 'thank you,' you'll get more."
- "I will do something else for you when I get a feeling that you appreciate what has already been done."
- "I don't do things for people who don't appreciate it. If it does not matter to you, I'll save my effort."
- "It seems like you think we have to do this for you. We really don't, and if it doesn't matter enough to you to show it, we'll stop."

You are expressing your own limits in not allowing yourself to be taken for granted. If you are truly feeling like a martyr, or a person who has suffered a lot and deserves pity, make sure that you deal with that feeling first so that you are letting the child know about his behavior without guilt.

Distinguishing Between Envy and Desire

One of the neat things about being a parent is helping your child achieve a desire. How wonderful to help a child reach a goal or attain something he wants! A friend's nineteen-year-old son recently purchased a car he had been working and saving for for three years. Every summer he worked and saved the money. After school he worked and put the money away. All along the way he and his parents had planned and prayed together, and finally the day came when he had enough money.

The car he purchased was a sports utility vehicle that suited all his interests. He has a ministry with kids on the beach, and he is also really into sports. The vehicle fit his *real person*. This was part of the reason he and his parents were both so into achieving the goal. And when he got it, it was a glorious day of thanksgiving and celebration.

Another teenager I know was given a new car without earning it and for the wrong reasons. It had nothing to do with the real person the daughter was. Her parents purchased the car to satisfy their own ego and to make their daughter compare well with other kids at school. It was not long before the car had lost its value to the girl, and she wanted another one.

One car was bought in response to a desire that came from the depths of a real person, and the other was purchased basically out of envy. Parents would do well to determine which wishes come from envy and which are heart-felt desires. Let the envious ones die, and help the child to achieve the ones that come from the heart. They last longer in the wanting, and longer after they are received. The ones from envy are lustful, comparative in nature, and short-lived in their ability to satisfy the child. As Proverbs says, "A longing fulfilled is sweet to the soul" (Proverbs 13:19). Lust has a continual craving for more.

It's Your Yard

When a child looks at the world outside himself and sees things he wants, this can be a good thing. His desire drives him to work. "The laborer's appetite works for him; his hunger drives him on" (Proverbs 16:26). When a child looks at his abilities, his possessions, or his skills and feels sad at what's missing, this also can be a good thing. His lack motivates him to goal-oriented activity. Thus, he learns the difference between envy and desire. Desire moves him to work. Envy just burns within.

If you have good limits and boundaries, you will empathize with your child's longing, help him to plan to reach the goal, and encourage him. If you don't give in to his envy, you have taught him a crucial lesson in life: His lack is his problem. If he does not like his life, he has to persist in praying to God and working as hard as he can to make it better. He has to realize that if he invests and grows his talents, God will participate and give him more (see the parable of the talents, Matthew 25:14–30).

In a person not dominated by envy, the thought process goes like this: "I see something out there I would like to have; I don't like my current situation. This is my problem. What am I going to do to get from point *a* to point *b*? I'd better pray, listen to God, evaluate what is keeping me from getting there, and find out what I need to do to reach that goal."

The key shift that has taken place in the child is that his wants and desires are his problem. He can ask for help, pray, learn, work, or whatever he needs to do. But his lack and the solution are his problem before God. No one should solve things for him. If this is happening, you are rearing a child who will find his true desires, seek God for the resources, abilities, and talents to get there, and reach out to his community for the learning and support that will be needed along the way.

The Paradox

Envy is a huge paradox in life. Envious people think they deserve everything, but in the end have nothing. They are not able to own, cherish, or be thankful for the things they possess. What they do not possess, possesses them.

Envy is basically pride, the feeling that you are God and that the universe belongs to you. But, as James tells us, pride loses in the end: "God opposes the proud but gives grace to the humble" (James 4:6). Humble people are those whose entitlement has been broken. They have been humbled, have received, and are thankful for what they have. In that kind of stance, God and others are most likely to give them more. This is the paradox. The envious want more, and get less. The grateful are thankful for what they already have, and receive more.

Help your child to become a humble, grateful person. But remember, swallowing the pride sandwich is a big bite and can only be done with a lot of love to wash it down. Then your child can get busy being active to solve his problems, which is the subject of the next chapter.

— 12 —

Jump-starting My Engine
The Law of Activity

After I (Dr. Townsend) graduated from college, I worked at a children's home in Texas for a couple of years. Six to eight school-age kids lived with houseparents in a cottage. We houseparents would cover each others' shifts to give each other breaks during the usually very stressful week. Because we all lived near each other, we got to know one another pretty well.

As a new houseparent, I observed differences between us. Basically, there were two extremes. The "best friend" type wanted more than anything for the kids to like him. He would spend lots of time talking to the kids and taking them to fun places in his car. He had a hard time being firm, not wanting to jeopardize his positive relationship with the kids. When it came time for inspection, his cottage was always a mess. Chores such as dishes, meals, and cleanup were done by him. The kids were pleasant, friendly, and lazy. They spent a lot of time on the couch watching TV.

The "control freak" type came in like an army drill instructor. He would bark orders from day one, set down consequences even before there were any problems, and generally run the kids around. His cottage was always well run and neat. The kids would grumble a lot, but they did their jobs for him. Every now and then a teenager would rebel and run away. The rest were pretty active and busy.

The best houseparents were somewhere in the middle; they were both relational and structured. The rule of thumb for success was this: *When respect came before friendship, activity*

resulted. When friendship came before respect, passivity resulted.
Friendship brought positive feelings, but also laziness. When
it came time for work, the kids resented the houseparent no end.
The houseparents who started with respect got more activity out
of their kids. Then, when they lightened up a little and had fun,
the children worshiped them.

The Bible teaches the same thing about our growth and the
growth of our children. First, we are self-centered and passive
about taking responsibility. We need the law (limits and consequences) to get our attention; law is for the lawless (1 Timothy
1:9). Then, when we realize that we aren't God and that passivity
will bring us pain, we get busy working on life, and God gives us
grace to help and support us.

The Gift of Activity

One of the greatest gifts you can give your child is to help build
in her a tendency toward activity. To be active is to take initiative, to make the first move. A child needs to understand that
the solution to her problems and the answer to her needs always
begins not with someone else, but with her.

Life requires activity in order for us to survive and succeed.
The first cry your child makes at birth is something that no one
else can do for him. When you hear this cry, you then do your
part in this process and respond to his need. All the way through
life, the onus of responsibility is on the child to take the initiative in solving his dilemmas, even though, especially in the early
years, he is deeply dependent upon his caretakers for the
resources to live.

Do not confuse dependency with passivity. We are designed
to be actively dependent on God and others all our lives. *By
the same token, do not confuse activity with self-sufficiency.*
Active people don't attempt to do everything on their own. Activity means doing all you can do, then aggressively seeking that
which isn't in you, to complete you. The Bible teaches this as
a collaboration between us and God. We have our tasks, and
he has his: "Work out your salvation, . . . for it is God who works
in you" (Philippians 2:12–13). Your child needs to actively let

his needs be known, protest the bad, hold up his end of his friendships, do his chores and schoolwork, and gradually shoulder more and more of the load of his life as he matures.

Children who are active have an ideal chance of learning to respond to boundaries correctly. Like an untamed bronco, they use their wills to buck against your limits and consequences until they learn to pay attention to realities other than their own. They encounter a few "owees" in life. Then they finally bend the knee to God's reality and start learning to tame their aggression, keeping it within acceptable limits and using it for constructive purposes.

God's gift of activity has many benefits for your child. It helps him to:

- Learn from failure and consequences how to behave appropriately
- Experience that his problems and needs are his to work out
- Develop a sense of control and mastery over his life
- Depend on himself to take care of himself
- Avoid situations and relationships that are dangerous
- Move toward relationships to get comfort and assistance
- Structure his love and emotions in a way that keeps him connected to God and others in meaningful and productive ways

The Bible confirms this Law of Activity over and over again. We are to carry our cross daily (Luke 9:23). We are to be diligent (Proverbs 12:24). We are to seek his kingdom and righteousness (Matthew 6:33). We are to knock on God's door as did the widow who needed assistance (Luke 18:1–5). We are to ask for what we need (James 4:2). As God himself is an active, problem-solving, initiative-taker, so we, made in his image, are to be.

The advantages of active children are sometimes hard for parents to understand. Often when we are speaking on the topic of kids and boundaries, a mom will ask for help with a problem: "I set the boundaries of behavior for my child. But she keeps crossing them. What do I do?" The answer is, "That's what is supposed to happen. You are the parent. You have a job. Your job is to set the limits and enforce the consequences in love. She is the child. She also has a job. Her job is to test the limits many times with her active aggression and thereby learn about reality, relationship, and responsibility. It's the divinely ordered training system."

The Problem of Passivity

Passivity, or being inert or nonresponsive, is the opposite of activity and initiative. Passivity in children is a major obstacle to boundary development. Passive kids are in a holding pattern in life, waiting on someone or something. *When children are passive, they are no longer learning to be stewards of themselves.* They are learning to give control to someone else, someone who will act in their stead.

Passive kids are unable to make use of the trying-failing-learning process that teaches them boundaries. They never really step up to the plate; they don't fail, but they don't grow, either. They are often really nice kids, but when you are around them, it is hard to get a sense of who they are. They often have difficulty making friends and finding interests and passions, and they can be easily influenced or controlled by more aggressive friends. They go along to get along. They don't "get a life."

I am always saddened when I think about all the kids who slip through the cracks of life by way of their passivity. They grow up, grow old, and die, having never really been touched, nor touching anyone else deeply. Their passivity confines them to a Twilight Zone existence. What a tragic waste of a lifetime!

The passive stance isn't a virtue, but a failing. Evil grows in the absence of active limits. The passive person is an unwitting ally of evil by not resisting it. The Devil waits for opportunities, which passive people provide him with their passivity (Ephesians 4:27). God isn't pleased with the person who shrinks back (Hebrews 10:38). In the parable of the talents, the master was angry with the servant who was afraid and didn't invest his talent (Matthew 25:24–28). Don't, however, confuse passivity with patience, which is a positive trait, namely, restraining our impulse to do God's job for him (James 5:8).

The message of the Bible concerning activity and passivity is, as the Marines say, "A bad decision is better than no decision." This is why, all things being equal, active kids learn and mature more quickly than passive ones. It means the parent has more raw material to work with.

What Can You Do About a Passive Child?

Parents of passive children have a double problem. These kids have the same boundary problems of irresponsibility or resistance to ownership, but it's harder to engage them in the learning process. Here are some ways children exhibit passivity:

- *Procrastination.* The child responds to you at the last possible moment. He finishes school tasks late and "makes" you wait in the car for him to get ready for school or other meetings. When you ask him to turn the music down or set the dinner table, a normally energetic and quick-moving child slows his pace down immeasurably. He takes enormous time to do what he doesn't want, and little time to do what he wants.
- *Ignoring.* Your child shuts your instruction out, either pretending not to hear you or simply disregarding you. She keeps attending to her toy, her book, or her daydreaming.
- *Lack of initiative and risk-taking.* Your child avoids new experiences, such as meeting new friends or trying out a sport or artistic medium, and he stays in familiar activities and patterns.
- *Living in a fantasy world.* Your child tends to be more inward-oriented than invested in the real world. He seems happier and more alive when he is lost in his head, and he retreats there at the first sign of problems or discomfort.
- *Passive defiance.* The child resists your requests by looking blankly or sullenly at you, then simply doing

nothing. She is obviously angry or contemptuous of your authority, but shows you without words.

- *Isolation.* Your child avoids contact with others, preferring to stay in her room. Rather than confront, argue, or fight with you, she instead reacts against some problem you present by leaving you.

Passive kids aren't bad or evil. They simply have a particular way of approaching life that prevents them from gaining autonomy, self-control, or mastery. Nor are all passivity problems similar in nature. Kids have struggles in this area for several reasons. The following are some of the root causes, along with ways you can help your passive children develop the activity needed to gain their own boundaries.

Fear

Your children may be nonresponsive because of underlying fears or anxieties that paralyze them from taking initiative. Overwhelming fear causes children to take a protective and defensive stance toward the challenges of life:

- *Closeness.* Some children are afraid of being close and vulnerable with others. They feel shy, reserved, and awkward around other kids. They will avoid social situations where they feel exposed. Don't take the stance that this is a "learning style" or a "personality type." While some kids are naturally shyer than others, they still need to learn how to connect with other people. Make school, church, sports, arts, and other social activities a normal and expected part of family life. Don't get in between your child and his acquaintances, but be there before and after, so he can talk about the experience.
- *Conflict.* Some kids are actively involved when everything is going okay, but become afraid and passive around anger or conflict. They may be afraid of someone's wrath, or of physical harm. Don't promise them that they'll never feel pain. But do reassure them that, as far as you can help it, you won't let them be injured.

Normalize conflict and pain. A friend of mine took his daughter to karate lessons every week. The first few weeks he was embarrassed because she would cry and hang onto his leg at the beginning of every session. But he told her, "You have to go for three months. You don't have a choice. I'll bring you whether you are crying or happy. After three months you can choose whether you want to keep coming or not." By the end of three months she had earned her next level belt and decided to stay. Teach your child that conflict is okay and that she will survive it.

- *Failure.* Many kids these days suffer from perfectionistic conflicts. Afraid of making a mistake, they prevent themselves from taking initiative and thereby reduce the chance that they will fail. They also lose the opportunity to learn from their failures. Again, normalize failure, and let them know they don't risk loss of love from you. You yourself can fail in front of them—and laugh at yourself.

A family that is close to mine is a good "failing" family. When we have dinner with them, we don't get grandiose stories of every member's achievements. Instead, they talk about the times they risked and failed at work or bumbled up some friendship. And the kids are part of that scenario. Failure is their friend.

Inability to Structure Goals

Desire and goals help kids overcome their inertia: "A longing fulfilled is a tree of life" (Proverbs 13:12). When they face conflicts, children often sink into passive stances. These kids aren't lazy. Rather, they have problems thinking through what steps to take to get what they want. Their tolerance for frustration is generally low. They may be overwhelmed by the task of researching their first term paper, so they give up. Or they might end friendships when conflict arises, preferring to stay home.

Don't rescue your child from learning structure by allowing her to avoid it. Home shouldn't be a place where a child can hide from life. Require her to learn skills and tasks at home. Tell her you'll help her. Chores that have some complexity, such as cooking, cleaning, grocery shopping, yard maintenance, even home repairs, will help her develop confidence in her ability to perform. Then she can begin working on goals in which she is interested. There is nothing like having to choose between cleaning an oven and designing a science project!

Clairvoyant Expectations

A child may feel he shouldn't have to ask for what he needs, on the assumption that you should know before he asks. He is upset when you don't ask him the right questions, forget something he wants, or don't understand why he is unhappy. This is a mark both of very young children and of older children who are having trouble separating their sense of self from their parent's. Infants need a mom who can anticipate their needs; otherwise, their existence is in danger. But as children grow up, they need to let their needs be known clearly.

Let your child know you really want to help him meet his needs and solve his problems. But also tell him, "Even though I love you very much, I can't read your mind. If you don't use your words and say what you want, you will not get a response. That would be sad. But if you take the effort, I will do what I can to help you."

Conflicted Aggression

Some kids are not innately passive. They are aggressive in some areas and nonresponsive in others. For example, a boy may be functionally active; he gets good grades and is responsible at home. Yet he may be relationally passive and isolated from sustaining relationships. Or even within the functional arena, a straight-A student may not be lifting a finger to help out at home.

These kids have the necessary active, assertive ingredients, but they have difficulty accessing them in certain areas. They need your help in using their initiative in the parts of life with which they have conflicts. Don't buy into the notion that "That's just the way I am." Maturing into the image of God means that we are to work on all the important areas of growth and life, not just the ones in which we are gifted.

The rule of thumb here is "You don't get the goodies until you make real efforts in your problem areas." To earn his allowance, stay up late, or watch a favorite show, the isolated ten-year-old must invite a certain number of kids per week over for dinner or rollerblading. Life dictates that we must all learn to eat our vegetables before we get dessert.

Laziness

Sometimes kids are passive due to a sluggardly position in life. They can be caring—kind kids—but they have little "anticipatory anxiety," the anxiety that prods us to go to work, take care of our relationships, and maintain our car. The future holds no fear for them. They know someone else will take care of any problems that arise. They lack fear of consequences.

Generally speaking, at the root of most lazy kids lies an enabling parent. At some level, you are paying for their laziness. You may not be aware of it, but you could be requiring too little from them in relation to their maturity level and resources. Providing them a life of comfort does them no favor in readying them for the real world. For example, is running the household a team effort or a token effort on your children's parts? Is their income tied to performance at home and school? Do not wait for your child to volunteer for all this. Set up the system, and follow through with the consequences.

A friend of mine who grew up in a wealthy family told me that now that she is a mother of three, having her kids keep the house neat is a real struggle. She said, "I just never thought about these things. I took off my clothes in my room and left them on the floor. When I got back to my room, the maid had picked them up. But now that I have kids, everybody's clothes stay on the floor. I wish I wasn't having to learn this so late in life."

It's hard to be simultaneously a lazy kid and a good, active, and responsible student. Talk to another parent and ask whether she thinks you're doing too much and your child too little. You'll be surprised at how much kids are capable of.

Remember that kids will be as passive as you train them to be. This personal-growth saying applies especially to lazy kids:

Nothing happens until the pain of remaining the same is greater than the pain of changing. Or, as the Bible puts it, "The sluggard's craving will be the death of him, because his hands refuse to work" (Proverbs 21:25). Set limits and consequences with laziness today, and spare your child this sorrow.

Entitlement

A major cause of passivity in children is an entitled attitude, a demand for special treatment. Such children feel they deserve to be served by virtue of their existence. They wait for others to meet their needs and wants, and they are seldom grateful for what they get, for in their minds, it is to be expected, given who they are.

All kids have a certain amount of entitlement. (See chapter 11 for an in-depth discussion of entitlement.) Since the Fall, humans have resented the reality that we aren't God, and we have done much to try to change this fact. But when you give in to this attitude in your children, you help create children who are not ready for the real world. They may either become quite disillusioned and have difficulty functioning, or find someone to marry who will stroke their ego and shield them from reality.

Cynthia, mother of sixteen-year-old Sean, both of whom are friends of mine, saw signs of passivity in her son. He was handsome, had an IQ of about 140, and had lots of friends. But he flunked out of not only high school, but also trade school, due to a lack of attendance and performance. Cynthia thought Sean's passivity was due to his not being challenged enough in school, and maybe his laziness.

Much to her surprise, Sean's entitlement emerged in full flower one day out of the blue. He had missed the bus and needed a ride to his new school. Cynthia had to take time off work. In the car she told him her concerns about his chronic passivity and what it was costing him and the whole family. She told him how inconvenient it was to take him to school. Suddenly Sean wheeled around and said, "Hey, you have to take me! I'm the kid. It's your job. I deserve it!"

Cynthia stopped the car and opened the passenger door. "You are the kid," she said. "But that doesn't mean you deserve what you're getting. We'll talk when you get home." Stunned, Sean got out and walked the final mile to school. He was furious. But by the time he got home that afternoon, he was ready to talk.

Cynthia regretted giving in to her angry impulse. But even though her action may have been inappropriate, it did help Sean realize that his attitude of entitlement had been exposed and wasn't working very well for him—a small first step toward working through it.

God's solution for entitlement is humility: "In humility consider others better than yourselves" (Philippians 2:3). Your child needs to know that, while he has legitimate needs, he isn't entitled to anything. In fact, the worst fate for any of us is to get what we really deserve, for we have all sinned (Romans 3:23). Your kid needs things, as all children need things. But he is responsible to provide these things for himself. If your child's passivity is due to feelings of entitlement, you will need to help him by frustrating his grandiose feelings while satisfying his real needs. "Special" people can't be loved, as love requires being known in our bad parts as well as our good parts. They can only be admired for their good. The child must give up his demands for admiration to be able to be loved.

Don't go overboard in praising required behavior: "We have only done our duty" (Luke 17:10). But do go overboard when your child confesses the truth, repents honestly, takes chances, and loves openly. Praise the developing character in your child as it emerges in active, loving responsible behavior.

Clinical Issues

Sometimes childhood passivity can be a symptom of an underlying emotional disorder. Some types of depressions, for example, can cause children to withdraw into passivity to cope with their internal pain. Drug and alcohol problems can also lead to passive roles. If you suspect these issues, see a therapist experienced with kids your child's age and get a clinical opinion.

Principles of Developing an Active Child

Whether or not your child is naturally passive, you will need to take a role in helping her be a seeker and grower. You are the primary solution in enforcing the Law of Activity. She can't do this herself, and although she will probably not appreciate your efforts, it will pay off in her character growth. Here is what you can do:

Become an Active Person, Not Just a Parent

A child needs to internalize a model of someone who has a life of her own. The parent whose life is centered around her children is influencing them to think that life is about either becoming a parent or being forever served by a parent. Let your child know you have interests and relationships that don't involve her. Take trips without her. Show her that you take active responsibility in meeting your own needs and solving your own problems.

Work Through Any Enabling of Your Child's Passivity

Don't confuse your love with rescuing your child from himself. Ask yourself and people you trust whether you are stretching your child's growth muscles sufficiently. Are you avoiding setting limits in the academic, work, social, spiritual, and behavioral areas of your child's life? Are you afraid of discussing these problems because of possible conflict? Is your home a retreat from responsibility, or a place of movement and growth?

A forty-year-old professional friend of mine, who is a husband and a father, becomes a passive child when he goes home to visit his mother. He sits on the couch and watches TV while his mother serves him drinks and snacks. When his wife saw this, she understood why she was having problems getting him motivated at home. His new mom—his wife—wasn't measuring up to the old one. Remember 2 Thessalonians 3:10: "If a man will not work, he shall not eat." Love and grace are free. Most everything else must be earned.

Require Initiative and Problem Solving

Your child's tendency is to let you do all the work. It is your fault if you do it. Begin to say things like, "I'm sorry, but that's your responsibility. I hope you solve your problem; it sounds difficult, but I'm pulling for you." Many, many problems can be addressed this way, with kids from four to eighteen:

- "Mom, have you seen my shoes?"
- "Oh, no, I missed my ride to school!"
- "I'm short on my allowance. Can I get a loan till Friday to go to a movie?"
- "I'm so mad at you for grounding me!"
- "Sorry I'm late, what's for dinner?"
- "It's the night before my paper is due, and I can't type."

As you can see, you may be able to reclaim many hours of time and lots of energy with the response "It's your responsibility." Your overactivity may have severely increased your child's over-passivity. Helping him take initiative to shoulder his own load strengthens his character and matures him; and it helps you to not take on more than God intended for you.

Teach Your Child to Move Toward Relationship

One of the fruits of passivity is that not only is your child prevented from solving problems, but also she is prohibited from receiving the good resources God designed to help her live her life. Passive children often avoid relationships in general, as they are either waiting for someone else to do things or they do not want to ask for help.

Help the child see that relationship is the source of many things:

- Comfort in emotional pain
- Feeling loved inside, rather than alone or bad
- Fuel for being assertive and being sustained through life
- Information for solving problems
- Structure for growth

Teach her that relationship only comes to those who actively ask. Don't chase her down in the "What's wrong? Nothing" game. Say, "Sounds like you're having trouble, but I will wait to help you until you ask." I know a dad who realized he was playing this game; he saw that chasing his ten-year-old daughter down wasn't helping her. So the next time she was upset, he said the above words. She walked past him as he sat reading the paper, and she whimpered softly, but loud enough that he could hear. He kept reading. She literally walked around the chair twelve times! Finally, she realized that relationship wasn't going to happen until she moved toward it. She said, "Dad, I'm sad about school." And only then did he lovingly help her.

Make Passivity More Painful Than Activity

Parents often reinforce passive children, as they seem to be less trouble than active ones, and it gives the parents more time to deal with the loud kids. But don't let your child be comfortable in that role. He risks getting lost in the shuffle. Let him know that you prefer active mistakes to passivity. Tell him, "If you are trying and mess up, I will help you as much as I can. If you don't try, I'll still love you, but you are on your own." Praise and reward the child when he tries to set the dinner table and spills everything. But when he avoids the task, he loses dessert that night.

Allow Time for the Process to Develop

Kids who struggle with passivity tend to need more patience as they move into active living. They have spent much of their lives fearing and avoiding risk, failure, and pain. Their assertive parts are suspect to them and not perceived as helpful to their lives.

Don't expect your child to be a problem-solving dynamo overnight. Reward little moves, even when he then retreats. Generally, there comes a point when, if the process is working right, the child's assertive parts will become more integrated. Like an engine winding up, his activity level will increase. But his first steps will probably be halting ones. Remember how much patience God had to have with all your steps, and be gracious: "Encourage the timid, help the weak, be patient with everyone" (1 Thessalonians 5:14).

Conclusion

Your child needs you to be the loving, limiting, provoking agent who teases out his active parts. He will resist you and be angry with you. But just as the mother bird knows when to push the baby bird out of the nest, use your experience, judgment, and the help of God and others to help him take initiative to own his life.

In the next chapter, dealing with the Law of Exposure, you will learn how to help your child in being direct and clear with his boundaries rather than falling prey to gossiping and playing parents off each other.

— 13 —

Honesty Is the Best Policy
The Law of Exposure

I (Dr. Cloud) can still remember what happened that day when I was eight years old. I made a big mistake, but I didn't know it at the moment. I thought I was getting back at my sister, who was sixteen at the time. Opportunities for revenge were few and far between, and I was not about to let this one slip by.

Sharon and her friend were goofing around in the den when one of them threw a pillow and broke the overhead light. They quickly figured out a way to arrange the light in such a way that you could not tell it was broken. They thought that they were off the hook. Little did my sister know that she had a sociopathic little brother with a plan.

When my father came home, I could not wait to tell him what they had done. I told him that they had broken the light, and he asked me to show him. I led him into the den, not knowing that Sharon and her friend were still in there. I was caught. Here he was, asking me about the broken light, and there they were, watching me seal my fate as a tattletale. I do not remember what he did to them, but I can still recall what they did to me, and it was not pretty.

It would be years before I understood the principle involved in this incident. But on that day I understood the reality: *When you go behind someone's back, you can expect trouble in the relationship.*

One of the most important principles in relationship is direct communication and full disclosure of whatever is going on in the relationship. I had never communicated to my sister what

I thought about what she did, given her a chance to turn herself in, or even cared enough to find out if she planned to tell Dad in her own time. My actions had two overriding motivations: I wanted my sister to pay, and I was afraid to be direct with her. I was foolish enough to think that I could pull it off without her knowledge and that I wouldn't have to deal with her anger.

Since I have become a psychologist, I have learned a lot about the destructiveness of indirect communication. This is how it happens. I have a problem with person a, and I tell person b. Now I have three problems: The first one that I told person b about, the second one of person b having feelings about person a that a doesn't know about, and the eventual problem of person a finding out that I told b and feeling betrayed by me.

The cousin of that dynamic occurs when person a tells me something about person b and then I tell person b. B is angry with a, and a does not know why. Later, a is mad at me for telling b, or in denial that he ever said anything to me in the first place.

The Bible says much about this kind of indirect communication of truth and also about the restorative value of direct communication. Here is a sample of how God feels about our not being honest in communication:

> He who conceals his hatred has lying lips, and whoever spreads slander is a fool (Proverbs 10:18).
>
> Rebuke your neighbor frankly so you will not share in his guilt (Leviticus 19:17).
>
> When I say to a wicked man, "You will surely die," and you do not warn him or speak out to dissuade him from his evil ways in order to save his life, that wicked man will die for his sin, and I will hold you accountable for his blood (Ezekiel 3:18).
>
> Therefore each of you must put off falsehood and speak truthfully to his neighbor, for we are all members of one body. . . . Do not give the devil a foothold (Ephesians 4:25, 27).

Being indirect in our communication can show us to be foolish, make us a part of the problem, make us accountable for the existence of the problem, and cause us to get caught up in the Devil's snare as we bury anger and strife.

Along with being against indirect communication, God also has much to say about the importance of direct communication in relationships and resolving things with another person:

> If your brother sins against you, go and show him his fault, just between the two of you. If he listens to you, you have won your brother over (Matthew 18:15).

> Therefore, if you are offering your gift at the altar and there remember that your brother has something against you, leave your gift there in front of the altar. First go and be reconciled to your brother; then come and offer your gift (Matthew 5:23–24).

> Better is open rebuke than hidden love (Proverbs 27:5).

Direct communication is the best way to go through life. But many people do not deal with others in that fashion. Instead, they practice avoidance (ignoring the person or the problem) or triangulation (bringing in a third person) or overlooking.

The Law of Exposure says that life is better lived in the light— that is, things are better out in the open, even if these things are negative. Whether the news is bad or not, we need to know it. Conflict or hard feelings cause a break in the connection between two people, and relationship can only be restored by communicating honestly.

This does not mean that we need to bring up every slight or everything that bothers us. Half the time, our irritation may be our problem anyway. Few things are more annoying than the person who always says, "We need to talk." As Proverbs tells us, "A man's wisdom gives him patience; it is to his glory to overlook an offense" (Proverbs 19:11).

But where values are violated or someone is injured or behaving unacceptably, then overlooking, avoiding, or triangulating causes more problems in a relationship.

In addition, people need to actively communicate their needs, wishes, desires, and feelings. Children who are shy or passive about asking for what they need must be helped to learn to initiate and to ask for what they want (see chapter 12). The withdrawn child who is wanting to be noticed or comforted needs to learn how to actively bring those feelings to relationship.

Let's look at some principles that will help your children to be open and honest in their relationships.

Rule # 1: Live the Law of Exposure Yourself

I was visiting a colleague's house recently, and his twelve-year-old son seemed particularly busy vacuuming, picking up things he had left around the house, and taking clothes to the washroom. I had not seen him so industrious before, so I asked him what was going on.

"I think I am in trouble," he said. "So I'm cleaning up. Maybe that's what it's about."

"What do you mean, 'Maybe that's what it's about'?"

"Well, when my mom was on the phone, I could tell that she was in one of her moods. So I'd better be careful."

"What did you do?"

"I don't know. But I know it was something."

"How do you know that?"

"Well, you can just tell. She's not her regular self."

It turned out that his mother was upset, but not with him. She was upset with her husband. The sad thing, though, was that the child was living with more than a little anxiety thinking that he had done something, but not knowing what. I thought that this was sad, so I asked his dad about it.

The story I got was that his wife would not ask people directly for what she wanted, and she would not tell them what they had done wrong. As a result, she could change the entire atmosphere of the house. All that they would know was that she was in "one of her moods." It was up to them to figure out who had done what.

This behavior was teaching her son some very harmful patterns. First, he was insecure with his own behavior. He did not know when he was doing well or failing. Second, he was not free to love. He was too busy worrying about his mom's feelings and having to take care of her moods and indirect communications. Third, he was seeing and modeling patterns of communication that would ultimately be harmful to his ability to have good relationships.

The way parents communicate, both with each other and with their children, is the starting point for the Law of Exposure. Live out what you want your children to learn. When you are upset or have a conflict with them, go to them and tell them—lovingly, but honestly and directly.

Rule #2: Make the Boundaries Clear

A child cannot develop a structured personality in a home where the rules and expectations are not clearly defined. When you have expectations and rules for your children, make sure they know them. This will give you opportunities for "training moments."

Training moments occur when both parents and children do their jobs. The parent's job is to make the rule. The child's job is to break the rule. The parent then corrects and disciplines. The child breaks the rule again, and the parent manages the consequences and empathy that then turn the rule into reality and internal structure for the child.

But training can't occur if the rule is not clear. The process breaks down. Make sure your children know what doing wrong is so you can teach them how to do right. As the Bible says, the law is a tutor to show us that we are lawbreakers (see Galatians 3:24 NASB). It's the same for kids.

Rule #3: Cure Their Fears and Make Communication Safe

The basic reason we do not communicate directly is that we are afraid. In general, two fears keep us from being honest: fear of loss of love and fear of reprisal. We fear that if we are honest with our anger or our hurt, the other person will either withdraw from us or be angry. In addition, children think that their anger is much more powerful than it really is, that it has the power to destroy you. They need to learn that you are bigger than their feelings so they can learn to be bigger than their feelings as well.

These two fears are universal. But they are reinforced in families where the fears are actually realized. I have worked with many adults who, when they are on the verge of being honest about something they feel, will cringe in panic and fear. In fact, this dynamic is at the root of a lot of adult depression and anxiety problems.

As a parent, you can either cure this universal sickness in your child or reinforce it. See the chart on the following three pages for examples of how you can reinforce the fear or cure it.

The key principles of this rule are these:

- All feelings are acceptable, and expressing feelings is a good thing.
- Expression of these feelings, however, has certain limits. For example, "I am angry with you" is okay. "I hate you" is okay." But "You are an idiot" is not okay. Hitting and throwing things are not okay, either.
- Empathize first to make a connection. First contain, accept, and love the children's feelings, then seek to understand.
- Self-control is the most important element. Children are out of control at this point, and they need your structure.
- Guard against splitting your love and limits. Be kind and loving, but remain strong enough to let them know that their feelings have not destroyed you or driven you away.
- Leave your pride, ego, and narcissism somewhere else. Reactions from those parts of you will reinforce your children's most primitive fears.
- After the conflict, have some good bonding time, even if it is just communicating affection. This lets them know the connection is secure even in conflict.
- Put words with feelings. Children are responsible for their feelings; putting words to feelings adds structure to them and makes them smaller than ultimate reality. If we can name and explain our feelings, they are just feelings. They are no longer global realities. Feeling sad is different from feeling as if the world is ending.

Incident	How to Reinforce the Fear	How to Cure the Fear
Child is angry at limit.	• Get angry back. • Attack his expression of anger. • Make him feel guilty for feeling angry. • Give him the silent treatment. • Act really devastated by his feelings. • Compare him to good children.	• Empathize with the anger. • Empathize with the frustration of having a limit and losing his wish. • Help him put words to his anger. • Stay soft and loving, but firm. • Keep the limit. • Limit expression that is attacking or inappropriate (at a later time when the feeling is past).
Child is upset with something you did wrong to her.	• Act injured by the accusation. • Give her some line about "How dare you question me?" • Blame back. • Withdraw love. • Get angry and overpower her.	• Empathize with the pain she's feeling. • Listen attentively and be open to the child's feedback about your behavior. • Help her to put into words what she did not like about what you did. • If you really were wrong, own it and apologize. • Ask her to let you know if you do it again. (This let's her know her complaint was taken seriously.) • If you did nothing wrong, say that you understand, but you don't really see what you did wrong. But thank her for telling you.

Incident	How to Reinforce the Fear	How to Cure the Fear
Child is hurt by life.	• Tell him to stop his whining, and call him a crybaby. • Tell him to stop crying or you'll give him something to cry about. • Make fun of him. • Compare him with his sister or a friend. • Call him a sissy.	• Empathize with how he feels. • Give understanding and comfort. • Help him put words to the hurt and the incident. • Don't be too quick to correct or explain reality. That can come after the emotions have passed. • Require him to work out his problem with his friend. Don't become the buffer between him and the outside world, giving him comfort and enabling him to avoid conflict with others. • Empathize and understand, but don't gratify his wish to use the hurt as an excuse to not get back into life or fulfill his requirements. Expression is good; withdrawal from life is not. At some point, the old admonition to "get back on the horse" is good advice.

- Keep lessons out of the interaction until you know your children have dealt with their feelings. Otherwise, they are not listening.
- The main guiding principle is this: *Our relationship is bigger than this conflict, feeling, or experience.* Our connection and affection will remain after this conflict is past.

Rule #4: Don't Reinforce Non-Expression

I was treating four-year-old Susie for childhood depression and trauma. Susie's parents were concerned with her gradual withdrawal into fantasy. Sometimes her feelings got hurt by something I said in our play, or she felt something and would not express it. At these times she withdrew from me and just played with the toys. But at the same time, I could tell she was watching me to see what I would do. I could also feel a pull from her to give in to her mood.

When this happened at home, her mother would usually ask Susie what was wrong, Susie would not say, and her mother would make an assumption about what was wrong and then give something to Susie. "You seem sad. Let's go get a cookie."

One day I decided to deal with Susie's feelings directly, and I was surprised at the fight I had on my hands.

"Susie, you seem quiet. What's going on?" I asked.

"Nothing," she said.

"Well, I don't believe you."

Shrug.

"I think that I'll just sit here until you tell me," I said.

"Fine. Can I go now?"

"Nope."

What came next was an intense exchange. I would not let her go, and she became more and more angry. Then she would catch herself, realize she was revealing feelings, and try to go stoic again. But I would not let her go. I was going to keep the limit until one of us grew old and died.

"I will sit here until you talk to me," I told her, and I just stared at her.

Finally, she began to tear up without really crying.

"You seem sad," I said.

She began to cry more. As she did, I comforted her, and the words came. She told me of the mean things that had happened to her.

That day, a bridge was built between me and her blocked-off inner world. But more important, she had experienced being required to be honest and direct about her experience instead of passively acting it out and wishing for someone to rescue her. Soon her parents learned how to require her to be direct and honest, and her patterns changed.

Generally, withdrawn and defiant children are afraid. Staying soft and loving, but at the same time not giving in to their non-expression will let them know that you are on the side of their fear and pain, but not on the side of their way of handling it. "Use your words" is a sentence some parents find helpful with small children who are non-expressive. A child's behavior will not change in a day. Remember the two ingredients: showing affection and requiring communication.

In my example, I waited Susie out, and the limit of not allowing her to leave finally broke the silence. Sometimes, however, you will have to be more active about pursuing the feeling. Interpreting the silence or asking questions helps. "It seems like you are mad right now." "It seems like you are sad right now." "I think you might be upset with me." Or just continuing to ask them to let you know what is bothering them and requiring them to express their feelings is helpful.

Other children communicate with actions, such as tantrums, yelling, name-calling, and running away. The trick is to disallow this form of expression and encourage verbal communication. "I want to know what you are feeling, but I want to hear you tell me instead of show me."

Rule #5: Don't Get in the Middle

As we said before, triangulation is putting someone else in the middle instead of dealing with the person with whom we have a problem. Don't let your children put you in the middle. When one sibling tattles on another is a great opportunity to teach this rule. Another is when a child is having a conflict with one parent, but telling the other, or asking one parent, getting a no, and then asking the other.

In general, except when it is unsafe, children need to work out their own conflicts. Let them solve their problems themselves. "I don't know why you are telling me. You need to work it out with your brother. He's the one you're mad at." Or, "Go work it out with your sister first. If the two of you can't settle it, then I might talk to you." Do whatever you can to keep the conflict between *them* so they learn the necessary conflict resolution skills.

The same principle applies to the other parent. If it is safe, get children to deal with him or her. If the conflict is with friends, let them work it out. This is what they are going to have to do later in life. Talking with them about how to do conflict resolution is okay, but requiring them to do it is important. The same goes for their problems with the school and other authorities. Certainly, there are times for conferences and meetings. But take every step to have your children work out the problems they are having with the school or organization. If Mom and Dad are always there to step in with authorities and "fix" it, the child will be lost when her first employer is upset with her performance.

Rule #6: Teach Them Boundary Words to Use

We have difficulty knowing what to say when we have conflict with others. We learn what to say over time, but it is a good idea to teach your children what to say and even role-play how they will say things to others when they need to set limits. They are dealing with peer pressure, hurtful kids, and strong personalities on the playground. If they are prepared, they will fare better. Here are some examples of tools to arm them with:

- "No." Period. Teach them how to say it.
- "No, I don't feel comfortable with that."
- "No, I don't want to."
- "No, I won't do that."

- "No, my parents don't allow that."
- "No, God does not want me to do that."
- "No, I learned that we don't touch each other's private places."
- "No, I don't like drugs. They kill people."

These words sound simple and somewhat trite. But some children need to know the words ahead of time and have some practice on how to use them. Role-play with them, or find some setting or group for them that does this kind of reinforcing of boundaries.

Bring It to Relationship

The ultimate boundary is love. Our connection with each other and with God is the fabric that holds life together. The truth we live and communicate gives this connection and love its structure.

Everything is ultimately about relationship. As Jesus said, all of the "boundaries" in the world can be summed up in these two laws: "Love God" and "Love your neighbor as yourself." For this reason, your child must learn to take his feelings, fears, thoughts, desires, and all of his other experiences into relationship. And if those conflicts have to do with a specific person, they need to work it out with that person whenever possible.

Relationship heals, comforts, and structures our experience. We need to learn that the love we need is bigger than what we are feeling, and the only way to find this out is to take what we are feeling to the relationship. Be the kind of person with whom your children can do this. Require them to do it with others. And they will be much less afraid of both their experiences and love itself.

Part 3

Implementing Boundaries with Kids

— 14 —

Roll Up Your Sleeves

The Six Steps of Implementing Boundaries with Your Kid

Whether you are a parent, relative, teacher, or friend of children, we hope you have gained some understanding about the importance of helping children develop their own boundaries and respect the boundaries of others. However, concern and insight, though necessary, aren't enough. If you put this book on a coffee table or under your child's pillow, it won't do him a lot of good. It is time to get to work.

In this chapter you will learn six steps of boundary implementation with your child. However, you need to understand this in context. This chapter is useless if you aren't setting boundaries yourself. As we have said in many ways, children need more than a parent who will talk about boundaries. They need a parent who will *be* boundaries. This means that in whatever situation arises, you will respond to your child with empathy, firmness, freedom, and consequences. This is how God handles his children, and he is our model.

A great deal of parenting involves responding to children's requests or problems:

- Saying no to demands for things they shouldn't have
- Addressing school problems they bring in
- Resolving power conflicts with you or their siblings
- Solving issues of lateness and messiness
- Helping with peer problems
- Working with dangerous issues, such as drinking, drugs, sex, or gangs

However, it's often helpful to have a structure in mind to proactively address boundary problems with your child. Using the following steps will help you avoid wasting time and energy going down rabbit trails while you try to figure out what to do next.

Remember, you aren't establishing a partnership with a peer. You're getting ready for battle with someone who isn't at all interested in cooperating with you. But nobody said parenting was a way to be popular!

So, on the one hand, don't begin this process by asking the child's permission or making sure she approves of the plan. On the other hand, don't begin in a reactive or authoritarian manner. Some parents have allowed themselves to be imprisoned by their kid's lack of structure. Then, when they realize that they have permission to be in charge, they go a little crazy to make up for all that lost time. They sit the kid down and read him the riot act, making the fatal mistake of saying, "From now on, you will and won't do the following."

Boundaries with kids isn't about "making" your child do anything. People who are coerced to do something don't have the freedom to make mature or moral choices. It is much more about structuring your child's existence so that he experiences the consequences of his behavior, thus leading him to be more responsible and caring.

Step 1: See the Three Realities

You need to come to terms with three realities. First, *there really is a problem: Your child is not perfect.* This reality may be manifested in a small way, involving some fine-tuning of behaviors or attitudes, or in a large way, involving the police. But all kids are immature sinners; this is our human condition. Some parents have difficulty with this first step. They deny their child's behavior. They rationalize genuine problems. Smarting off becomes a cute sense of humor. Laziness becomes fatigue. Intrusiveness becomes high-spiritedness. If someone else has given you this book and you don't know why, ask the five most honest friends you have and see what answers you get. As the saying goes, "If one person calls you a horse, tell them they're nuts. If five tell you, buy yourself a saddle!"

Parents rationalize their child's problems for many reasons. Some do it to avoid guilty feelings. Some don't want their own perfectionism challenged. Some feel as if their child is being victimized. Others don't want to be embarrassed. Still others don't want to go through the effort of disciplining. Parents need to look at the possibility that they might be sacrificing their child's well-being to protect their own sense of comfort and well-being. God never denied our craziness, and he went through the ultimate discomfort to solve the problem. Be a parent.

After admitting the problem, the second reality to come to grips with is that *the problem isn't really the problem.* The behavior or attitude driving you crazy isn't the real issue. It is the symptom of another issue, which in many cases is a boundary problem. Your child's behavior may be driven by something broken or undeveloped within her character. The symptom alerts you to the inner problem. Don't just react to the symptom, or you will be guaranteeing more problems later. Parents often have a knee-jerk reaction in a crisis, then back off from their job when the crisis resolves. A boundaryless child will have symptoms until she develops boundaries.

Here are some examples of problems that aren't the problem:

Outward Problem	Boundary Problem
Bad grades	Lack of concern about consequences
Controls other kids	Lack of respect for others' boundaries
Doesn't listen to instruction	Lack of fear of consequences
Defiant attitude	Lack of boundaries on entitlement

The third reality you will need to come to terms with is that *time does not heal all.* Many parents will avoid addressing boundary problems because someone told them, "Just wait it out.

They'll get older." They will get older. But how many forty-two-year-olds do you know who are getting older but still have no boundaries? Time is only a context for healing. It is not the healing process itself. Infections need more than time; they need antibiotics.

In fact, avoiding dealing with problems in your child simply gives the Devil more opportunity to stunt his growth (Ephesians 4:27). Time is a necessary but not sufficient condition for boundary growth and repair. You also need lots of love, grace, and truth for your child. Get involved in the repair process. With nothing but time, things do not improve, but break down further.

Step 2: Plug In

Make sure you connect to good, supportive relationships outside of yourself, even in addition to your spouse. Helping your child with boundaries ultimately helps his emotional and spiritual growth, but growth never occurs in a vacuum. This work is exhausting and frustrating; it can even drive you crazy. Information isn't enough. You will need much love and help from others.

Many parents lose the boundary battle simply because they have been worn down by an actively resistant child who understands what he is about to lose and puts up all sorts of obstacles. He will use his wits to make you feel that you're being unfair or hurtful. Your realities and resolve will be sorely tested. If they're all alone, with work and marriage responsibilities, parents throw up their hands and say, "You win." But with people who won't condemn you, who will walk with you through the fire, and who will hold you accountable to do the right thing, you can stick by your guns. If you could do it alone or just with your spouse, you probably would have by now.

Find or start a parenting group, a Bible study that works on boundaries issues, or a neighborhood group. Use it to trade tips, secrets, techniques, and victories and failures. You may want to use the *Boundaries with Kids Workbook* to help you structure the learning experience. Our church has a group for parents of kids who are our kids' ages. The pastor of this ministry is very vulnerable about his own struggles as a parent. He helps make it politically incorrect *not* to have kid problems. Parents in denial come out frustrated, which is what they need. Normal parents come out relieved that they aren't nuts and that there is hope. "In abundance of counselors there is victory" (Proverbs 11:14 NASB).

Step 3: Grow in Boundaries Personally

Before you start preaching boundaries to your child, start walking the walk. Kids are able to sense deception amazingly well. They haven't been on the planet long enough to lie sufficiently to themselves about what they see. They know when you are being a hypocrite or telling them to do something you won't. But even more than that, all of us simply need to be developing and clarifying our boundaries for life anyway.

We have known many parents who have used the boundary conflicts and heartbreaks with their children as an opportunity to grow spiritually and emotionally themselves. Few things can bring us to our knees more quickly than an out-of-control child. This humbling, hurtful, and overwhelming reality forces us both to look inside ourselves and to reach out to God and his resources.

This step invites you to work not only on your boundaries, but also on your life. You need to be doing the hard work of relating to God and growing spiritually, emotionally, and in good character. You need all that he has to help you live. You need friends who will comfort, support, and confront you on your own weaknesses and selfishness. It is hard for kids to grow when they aren't around growing parents. Don't be like the parents who look to church and school to help their children become mature. Your child is waiting for you to be a model of a seeking, honest person, actively involved in knowing God and others: "Blessed are they who keep his statutes and seek him with all their heart" (Psalm 119:2). If you want your farm to run right, it's wise to ask the one who made the farm how to run it.

Some parents begin working on their own boundary issues and find that they have a hard time saying no to their spouse, their boss, and their friends. They realize why their children run all over them. These parents get in a support group or good church and start strengthening their muscles. They begin taking more control over their lives, and they stop fearing conflict and guilt. All of a sudden, things begin to get better with their children. You may want to read for yourself our book *Boundaries*, which focuses on personal boundaries instead of specific parenting issues.

Or you may find that you have difficulty respecting others' boundaries. You may be an active, aggressive person who does not hear other people's no. Accept your helplessness, work on influence rather than control, and understand Jesus' empathic Golden Rule: Treat others the way you want to be treated (Matthew 7:12).

Once I (Dr. Townsend) worked with a dad and his teenage son, who was picking the wrong friends, ditching school, and using drugs. The father, who had a military background, couldn't understand why his controlling tactics weren't working.

One day they showed up at my office, and the boy's shoulder-length blond hair had been chopped off above his ears. The dad had impulsively taken the boy to a barber, who had shorn it. "I'm tired of all this psychobabble. I decided to solve the problem myself," he told me. "Now he isn't like those bad kids." The boy was enraged and humiliated.

"This move only made your real problems worse," I told the father.

It took a long time, during which the boy got into more trouble, before the father was able to see that he had to stop controlling and start allowing freedom and consequences to work. This dad had to do a lot of work on his own boundaries. In doing this, he allowed his son to be kicked out of a school he valued and even to be hauled into juvenile court for drug use. He supported his son's feelings, but he also supported the limits imposed by the authorities. Without nagging his son, the dad set up house rules with reasonable consequences that he then followed up on. In time, his son became more responsible, less impulsive, and more productive in school and work.

Step 4: Evaluate and Plan

Evaluate your child's situation and your resources, and develop a plan to deal with the problem.

The Child

Get to know your child's boundary problem in light of herself. Write out a list of several important factors:

Age. Toddlers look at life differently than teens, though most boundary problems are universal. Be aware of the normal issues of your child's age group, especially what she is capable of. The trick here is to push your child beyond her comfort level, but not beyond her abilities. Infants under twelve months, for example, should have a lot of nurture and few boundary expectations. At one year, you should begin training with the word *no* to behaviors such as crawling on furniture and sticking fingers into electrical outlets. The rule of thumb is that the older the child, the more frustration she can tolerate.

Maturity level. Maturity level varies from child to child; some six-year-olds are more grown-up than some seventeen-year-olds. Look at issues such as basic trust, ability to make and keep good friends, responsiveness to commands, ability to disagree and protest, ability to tolerate deprivation, ability to accept loss and failure in herself and others, and attitude toward authority. Seek the input of others who know your child, such as teachers, church friends, neighbors, relatives, and counselors. Below are what we believe to be the two most important character attributes your child needs in order to mature. If she has these, your work will go much easier. If there are problems here, work on these as you address the specific boundary problems.

- *Attachment.* Is your child able to connect emotionally to you? Does she see you as someone who cares for her? Or is she detached, distant, or chronically cold?
- *Honesty.* Does your child tell the truth? Or does she struggle with lying and deceit?

Context. What is her life setting? Are you divorced or is your marriage in trouble? Does she have any clinical issues (neurological, learning disorders, attention deficit disorder)? Are there problems with other siblings? Understand her environmental influences.

Specific boundary conflict. Isolate the specific boundary issue in your child's life. Is she having problems with family rules, chores, school, or friends? How can you state it simply?

Severity. Determine how profound the problem is. You may have a child whose biggest problem is that you need to tell her three times to do something before she does it. You will need to take a different approach with this child than with a child who is unable to sit still and is the subject of calls from school. Don't sweat the small stuff. Address issues that involve honesty, responsibility, caring, and morality. Give more latitude within limits to hairstyle, music, and room sloppiness.

Your Own Resources

Now that you are getting a more comprehensive picture of your child's boundary problem, where it comes from, and how severe it is, evaluate what you have at hand to deal with it. Look at the following factors:

Your own issues. As we have said, the most important thing is not what you do, but who you are with your child. Observe how you react, avoid, cajole, or ignore him. Be working on whatever is broken in you that causes you to respond inappropriately. To the extent that you see yourself as the child's external boundary, which he is internalizing, you are either the key to the solution or the perpetuator of the problem.

Your life context. Look at your life's realities, such as emotional struggles, marital conflicts, finances, job pressures, and other kids. If you are in crisis, get help for yourself quickly. We have seen many parents who had kids with boundary problems, yet they had overwhelming chaos in their marriage. First things first. Get in a position where you have enough order and structure to bring order and structure to your child.

Let me speak a word here to single parents: God designed the job of nurturing and rearing kids to two parents for several reasons: (1) The child is loved by two people who love each other;

(2) each parent brings different aspects of maturing to the child that the other may not have; (3) they serve as a check-and-balance system for parenting in which each corrects the other when he or she is off base in some area.

Single parents don't have this support and accountability. Many serve as both mother and father to their children and take on an enormous responsibility. In addition, single parents have their own problems—their ex, finances, work, time, dating, loneliness, and other stressors. If you are a single parent, you can't do it all alone, especially in having the energy it takes to deal with your child's boundary problems.

Take initiative to find help and resources. Many churches have ministries for single parents. Check with your community, neighborhood, relatives, and friends for help and assistance. Your child needs the involvement and specific functions others can bring—for example, a church youth group with healthy adult leaders who are the opposite sex from you, two-parent families who will take one of your kids to baseball games and dinners, or people who can help with homework, personal problems, sports, spiritual growth, and art.

We have seen many single parents with boundaryless kids turn their children in the right direction with the love and support of others in their lives. Remember that God, in a way, is also a single parent (Jeremiah 3:8). He was symbolically "divorced" from Israel and raised his family without her! He understands the struggle and will help you.

A boundary-resistant spouse. You may be married, yet alone in your determination to help your child learn boundaries. This can be a serious problem if the child puts one parent in the middle of his conflict with the other parent. In these settings, the "pro-boundaries" parent is often seen as the mean, depriving one and the "anti-boundaries" parent as the good, gratifying one. The child becomes divided within himself about responsibility and ownership and often plays to the gratifying parent to solve his problems.

If your spouse doesn't support boundaries, address this with him or her before you begin serious work with your child. If he or she is having the fun and you end up paying for the irresponsibility, rearrange things so that the boundaryless parent reaps the consequences. For example, if your spouse doesn't want to insist on the child's doing chores, don't do them yourself. Let your spouse do them. If your spouse doesn't want your child to stay home and do homework, refer the school calls to him or her to meet with the teacher. If the resistance is severe, you may have to seek marital help. In most cases like this, the boundary problems of the spouse are affecting more than the parenting. See this not as a parenting issue, but as a marriage issue.

The Plan

Come up with a structure that you will use for yourself and will present to the child. Based on the work you have done above, include the following aspects and write them down. This is important. Many parents have been caught in the "That's not what you said" routine. What is written down can't be questioned as easily. It may be a good idea to deal with only one or two boundary problems in the beginning if you haven't worked on this matter before. Remember that you're turning the rules of reality upside down (but in the right direction) for your child. At first, this may seem to her like living on an alien planet.

The problem. State the issue in specific terms. Your child's grades aren't acceptable. She has behavior problems: not listening to instruction, lateness, fighting, not following through on tasks. Or she has attitude problems: talking back, insults, rage attacks, tantrums, whining. When stating the problem, stay away from character attacks that the child then has to defend herself against, such as "You're a loser and a slacker."

The expectations. You want the grades to not be below a "B" average. You want her to respond the first time you ask. You want zero fights. Disagreeing is okay, insults are not. Make your expectations measurable. What is measured tends to improve more than what is not.

The consequences. Write what will happen when the child doesn't meet your expectations. The child will lose so many privileges, have so many restrictions—for example, losing evening or weekend time with friends, or TV and computer time. Set it up so that, as much as possible, the punishment fits the crime. Set up positive consequences, too, for success in meeting expectations. Be careful about the positives, however. Some parents go overboard in reinforcing anything that isn't savage-level behavior. You don't want to set up your child to think that she gets cookies or a new car every time she brushes her teeth. She will be sorely disappointed when she shows up for her first job and nobody gives her a party for coming to work on time. It's okay to set up minimum standards of behavior in the home with no reward.

Step 5: Present the Plan

You and your child both need to be a part of this process. The more you involve her in it, and the more time, help, and information she gets, the more likely she is to take ownership of it and cooperate in her own growth. Invite her to partner with you, even though the plan is still going to be executed if she refuses. Include the following elements:

Introduce the plan at a peaceful time. Pick a good time and place when you and the child are getting along. Don't pull out your papers in the middle of a screaming match. That only serves to polarize things, and the child often feels forced to react more strongly against you to maintain separateness.

Take a "for" stance instead of an "against" stance. Let the child know this process isn't about forcing her to do something or because you're angry. Tell her you see a problem that's hurting her and others in her life. You want to deal with it because you love her, and you want to do it together with her.

Present the problem. As we have said, make it specific. Talk about its hurtful effects on her and others: "Your yelling and running behavior is a problem. It's disruptive at home and at school, and it doesn't seem to be getting better."

Present the expectations. As above, make her a part of the process. Let her know exactly what standards you expect.

Present the consequences. Take a big breath and be direct. Don't be afraid of the bad news. You aren't hurting her; you're freeing her from herself! Emphasize her freedom in meeting your expectations. She doesn't have to do anything; she can choose to act as if you don't exist. The key is that *if she chooses to resist, the consequences will become a reality.* Remember: You can't control the behavior, but you can control the consequences. Stay in control of what is yours and encourage her freedom to choose.

Negotiate what is negotiable. Let the child have some input, within parameters, on expectations and consequences. Giving on something minor may pay off, as the child will feel less helpless and more involved in her destiny. Let her know that you may adjust something later if she proves herself for some period of time. Don't budge on the nonnegotiables, however. Drugs, alcohol, premarital sex, violence, failing grades, and truancy are not gray areas.

Remember also that adult rules are different from kid rules. Many times a child will protest, "You don't do that, why should I?" This happens in many contexts, including bedtime, finances, and free time. You do need to be humble enough to admit it if you are truly transgressing in some area, and then change your behavior. The reality is, however, that adults do have more freedom than kids, because they are (we hope) more responsible. Responsibility brings freedom. Tell your child about that. Hold it out as an incentive to accept the boundaries. Growing up has its rewards.

Make expectations and consequences easily accessible. A notebook, bulletin board, or posting on the refrigerator door is a good way to remind of expectations and consequences. As with any contract, both of you may need to refer to it often.

Step 6: Follow Through over Time

This last step is more difficult and more important than all the others. *The whole idea of a plan will fall apart if you are not personally functioning as the boundary for the child.* This all hinges on your doing what you say you will do. To paraphrase, the road to boundaryless hell is paved with good intentions. Here are some of the things with which you will need to deal:

Expect disbelief and testing. You are implementing a new way for the child to experience the universe, one in which her behavior and her suffering are directly associated with each other. She doesn't have a nagging or raging parent to focus on, ignore, or get around. She has an adult who is now standing back and letting her freely choose for herself how difficult or how pleasant her life will be. This will be an adjustment.

Although your child may argue with you when you present the plan, this is generally not the real test. At that stage she may see your presentation as nagging and tune you out. *It is when you enforce the consequence after she transgresses the boundary that you will see the resistance.* You can expect reactions like shock, disbelief, anger, expressions of hurt and woundedness, isolation, blaming, attempts to pit you against the other parent, and even escalation of the behavior. She is in the middle of a titanic struggle of integrating reality into her soul. And though she may be making *you* miserable, *she's* not happy, either. The war inside her is far worse than her war with you. Have compassion for that struggle: She is like a sheep without a shepherd, lost in her immaturity (Mark 6:34).

We cannot overemphasize how critical it is at this juncture to stick with the consequences. You may feel guilty, bad, abusive, hated, isolated, overwhelmed, and unloved. Hang on to the boundary! Pray, call friends for support, do whatever you can to stay with it. Remember that this is what God goes through with us every time he disciplines us for our own good. We protest, hate him, whine, shake our fist, and condemn him as being an unfair God. Yet he loves us enough not to let us call the shots and further ruin ourselves. Your consequence is a team effort by you and God for lovingly nurturing and training your child.

At this point it may be helpful to think back on your life. Reflect on those times when a lack of structure and consequences has cost you; remember when being overcontrolled, with no ability to choose, kept you handicapped in making decisions in life. Give your child the benefit of the hard lessons you learned about responsibility and reality by not protecting her from reality.

Be patient and allow repeated trials. Your child is on a learning curve, and learning takes many trials. Expect her not only to transgress the boundary, but also to protest the consequences many times. Be patient with yourself, too. If boundaries are new for you, you may not follow through all the time: "But solid food is for the mature, who by constant use have trained themselves to distinguish good from evil" (Hebrews 5:14). Stay with it and follow through as consistently as you can. If you find you are not able to do that, seek help from mature friends who may be able to explore with you whether the problem is one of resources, abilities, character, or unrealistic expectations. Then you can make adjustments.

Praise the child's adaptations. If the process works correctly, you will begin to see less of the bad behavior and more of the good behavior you're after. Your child may become sad as she experiences her own limitations and vulnerability. Be warm and validating with her. She is working very hard, though complaining the whole way, to integrate boundaries and adapt herself to your expectations. Don't focus on your love for her, as that should be a constant. Turn her focus more on how her life is more pleasant without the consequences and how others around her are happier, too. Help her to see that this is for her benefit, not to gain your love. Get with your support group and have a boundary success party.

Fine-tune and shift issues. When you feel the child is mastering the behavior and is more in control of herself, you may want to increase expectations. Or you may want to focus on another problem. However, the child shouldn't feel that the whole relationship is about boundaries. Make sure there are loving, fun, free times, too. But she does need to know that the tasks of growing up continue all the way through life, that she may "live a life worthy of the Lord and may please him in every way: bearing fruit in every good work, growing in the knowledge of God" (Colossians 1:10). You and she need to always be engaged in that process.

Am I Too Late?

An important question parents ask us about implementing boundaries is "Is it ever too late to start?" Parents who struggle with severe conduct problems in teenaged or adult children can be desperate and discouraged. We say it is never too late to begin doing the right thing for you and your child. Becoming more honest and clear about responsibility, taking more initiative to solve problems, and bringing a sense of structure to your home are all critical parts of your own spiritual and character growth, of a life lived in the light of God. Even if your child has no boundary issues, you still need to orient your life toward righteousness: "God is present in the company of the righteous" (Psalm 14:5).

At the same time, the younger the child, the easier it is to establish boundaries as normative. As the Bible teaches, youth is for training: "Train a child in the way he should go, and when he is old he will not turn from it" (Proverbs 22:6). The longer a child lives with the delusion that he is God, the more resistance he will have to giving up living in this happy place in his head.

Yet, children are still children, even in the teen years. *A child is someone who isn't an adult, meaning someone without the necessary skills and tools to navigate real life.* This means that, no matter what they say, they are incomplete and unfinished and will fail in life, except that God has built them to need you as the growing-up agent. That smart-alecky, distant kid needs you!

Some internal part of your child needs you to get involved and, amidst all his protests, take charge as a parent. He is often terrified of his own out-of-control emotions and behaviors and wants someone bigger than himself to help contain and structure his existence. Working with resistance and defiance is a fundamental part of parenting, and at some level, your child knows that.

Think about the issue as one of resources. If you have a teen, especially one with severe problems, you will need to bring more resources to bear on the situation. More time, effort, money, and institutions such as the school, the church, counseling services, and the court system may be needed. The parent of a seven-year-old may expend less effort, while that of an acting-out teen may spend many months and much energy working on these issues.

You may have to settle for incomplete results. A sixteen-year-old who has had a conduct problem all his life may not enter Harvard. But he may get some very important experiences with you that will help him grow through his last two years of childhood. He may also get a way of looking at how to conduct his life and handle his problems that will help him in adulthood.

Many teens whose parents have intervened late in life will seek growth and help in their adult years on their own. When you live in the nest, you are protected from the full consequences of life. Your biggest problem is your clueless parents. But when you start having to pay rent, buy food, and worry about pregnancies, you may see life in a different light. Many teens will then take to heart what their crazy mom and dad did with them those last years and start making boundaries part of their lives.

Don't give up on your child, even in the last years of adolescence. Use every opportunity, as the days are evil (Ephesians 5:16). You are the only mom or dad they will ever have; no one in the world has the position of influence in their heart that you do.

The Hope You Have

The words *parenting* and *problems* sometimes seem to be redundancies. You may simply be preventing problems in your child. Or you may have a troublesome situation that is breaking your heart. Yet, God has anticipated it, is fully aware of it, and wants to help you to help your child develop boundaries. He has provided hope for your and your child's future that is real and helpful. This hope comes in the following ways.

God Himself

As your child's heavenly Father, God is intimately concerned that your child mature into a person of love, responsibility, and self-control. God wants to help you as his agent in that process. Go to him in need and supplication, asking for all the guidance and resource he can provide: "With your help I can advance against a troop; with my God I can scale a wall" (Psalm 18:29).

His Statutes

God has provided principles and laws in his Word that outline the process of developing maturity in his people. This book is based on many of those realities. Use it and other resources, but even more, read and study his Word for a structure for life and parenting: "Remember your word to your servant, for you have given me hope" (Psalm 119:49).

His Reality

As God designed the universe according to his nature, life works better when we do it his way. When we are caring, responsible, and attuned to him, we have a better prospect of a good life. Reality is on your side. It is constructed so that immaturity causes your child some discomfort; ownership should bring some measure of satisfaction and fulfillment. Allow your child to experience both realities so as to learn boundaries: "Diligent hands will rule, but laziness ends in slave labor" (Proverbs 12:24).

His People

Safe people will help you help your child. Let them minister to you and him both, filling you up with love, structure, support, and guidance: "From him the whole body, joined and held together by every supporting ligament, grows and builds itself up in love, as each part does its work" (Ephesians 4:16).

Your Child

Believe it or not, your child is an agent of this same hope of growth and responsibility. God designed him with a need to learn to take ownership of his life in submission to him. He may not be aware of that need—but you are. Remember that you are helping to develop the image of God that is already in your child and is waiting to be strengthened: "So God created man in his own image, in the image of God he created him" (Genesis 1:27).

Use these sources of hope as a help, comfort, and tool as you walk in his ways, and train your child to do the same.

Thanks again for the sacrifices you make daily in parenting, and God bless you.

For information about Drs. Cloud and Townsend's books, tapes, resources, and speaking engagements, contact

Cloud-Townsend Communications
260 Newport Center Drive #430
Newport Beach, CA 92660
Telephone: 714-760-3112